# circuit hikes

## in shenandoah national park

1976
potomac appalachian trail club
washington, d.c.

# CIRCUIT HIKES
## in the
## Shenandoah National Park

Text by
James W. Denton

Maps by
The Maps Committee, Potomac Appalachian Trail Club
Egbert H. Walker, Chairman

Photos by
Bob Farr (page 83)
William S. Hall (pages 3 and 45)
Rafael Miranda (pages 59 and 79)
and *PA* Staff (pages 17, 29, 37, 55 and 69)

1976 Edition

Potomac Appalachian Trail Club
1718 N St., N.W., Washington, D.C. 20036

L.C. No. 76-21937
ISBN 0-915746-08-5

Copyright © 1976 by the Potomac Appalachian Trail Club,
Washington, D.C. 20036

# SHENANDOAH NATIONAL PARK
# CIRCUIT HIKES

Foreword ....................................................... v
Introduction .................................................. vii

| Hike No. | Title | Approximate Distance mi. | km. | Page |
|---|---|---|---|---|

## NORTHERN SECTION HIKES: PATC Map 9

| | | | | |
|---|---|---|---|---|
| 1. | Bluff Trail | (13) | (21) | 1 |
| 2. | Big Devils Stairs | (8 and 11) | (13 and 17) | 5 |
| 3. | Piney Ridge-Little Devils Stairs | (6 and 12) | (9 and 20) | 9 |
| 4. | Jeremys Run-Neighbor | (14) | (23) | 19 |

## CENTRAL SECTION HIKES: PATC Map 10

| | | | | |
|---|---|---|---|---|
| 5. | Hazel Country | (6 and 10) | (10 and 16) | 21 |
| 6. | Stony Man Mountain | (3 and 4) | (5 and 7) | 27 |
| 7. | Old Rag Mountain | (7) | (11) | 31 |
| 8. | Cedar Run-Whiteoak Canyon | (8 and 9) | (12 and 15) | 33 |
| 9. | Rose River | (9 and 10) | (14 and 17) | 39 |
| 10. | Dark Hollow | (4 and 6) | (6 and 10) | 43 |
| 11. | Hoover Camp | (10) | (16) | 47 |
| 12. | Lewis Falls | (4) | (6) | 49 |
| 13. | South River Falls | (4 and 10) | (7 and 16) | 53 |

## SOUTHERN SECTION HIKES: PATC Map 11

| | | | | |
|---|---|---|---|---|
| 14. | Rocky Mount | (10) | (16) | 57 |
| 15. | Rocky Mountain-Brown Mountain | (10) | (16) | 61 |
| 16. | Big Run Trail | (6 and 7) | (9 and 12) | 63 |
| 17. | Rockytop | (15 | (24) | 67 |
| 18. | Falls Trail | (7 and 8) | (10 and 13) | 71 |
| 19. | Austin Mtn.-Furnace Mtn. | (12) | (19) | 73 |
| 20. | Trayfoot Mountain | (9) | (15) | 77 |
| 21. | Riprap Hollow | (9) | (15) | 81 |
| 22. | Turk Branch-Moormans River | (9 and 21) | (14 and 34) | 85 |

# FOREWORD

*Circuit Hikes in the Shenandoah National Park* has been appearing in ever new versions over a good many years. It is the most popular of the guidebooks for hikers published by the Potomac Appalachian Trail Club.

The present edition, the tenth in the series, builds on the labors, unpaid and largely unsung, of many members—and some non-members—of the Club, most especially of the succession of editors of this publication. When Dave Banks, who edited the ninth edition, told us that he would be leaving our area and therefore could not work on a new edition, we were fortunate to recruit Jim Denton for this task. Jim and his wife, Molly, live in Front Royal practically on the doorstep of the Park. They know the Park inside out. Molly is the editor of the new edition of our *Guide to the Appalachian Trail and Side Trails in the Shenandoah National Park*. The two have worked as a team, and the Club has been wonderfully served by this happy arrangement.

This edition of *Circuit Hikes* marks a very substantial forward step over all previous editions. The text has been completely revised and brought thoroughly up to date (although, as Jim would be the first to say, there are so many developments in the Park that it is impossible to be totally accurate at any one time—and hikers would be well advised to bear this word of caution in mind). For the first time in any PATC guidebook we have actual hiking times spelled out for each trail, so that the hiker can more easily plan his outing. We have made a major advance towards the use of the metric system, in line with national trends. Differences in elevation over the course of a hike are set out in the text.

The maps that go with each hike are no longer just schematic drawings, as in previous editions. They show contours, exact distances, water courses and other essential features, and they are in two colors. The user of this little book has everything that is needed to inform on any particular hike, between its covers; however, the Club's three larger maps covering the Shenandoah National Park (Maps 9-11) will continue to be valuable additional resources for the hiker in the Park, as will our larger *Guide*.

The 22 maps in this edition of *Circuit Hikes* were produced over the course of four months by volunteer members of the Maps Committee under the general guidance and with the meticulous participation of its eminent chairman, Dr. Egbert H. Walker, who, as this publication goes to press, has retired from this position which he has held with distinction for several decades. Jordan D. Ross and Alan W. Withers had the principal role in creating these maps, and the latter owe their existence to many long hours and painstaking effort which these two PATC members gave to the enterprise.

The Shenandoah National Park is truly a jewel in the backyard, as it were, of the nation's capital. Increasing numbers of people are drawn to it to refresh minds and bodies in the beauties which it has to offer. All too few are aware that its attractions go well beyond the well-known (and by now all too well worn) trails over the top of Old Rag Mountain, and down White Oak Canyon. It is the ardent hope of the publishers of this book that it will encourage people to sample other lovely hikes in the Park. There is a great deal to be seen and experienced between the northern and southern ends, and the time has come to ease the load on the more popular trails.

Alexander F. Kiefer, *Chairman*
Publications Committee
July, 1976

# INTRODUCTION

In this revision of *Circuit Hikes in the Shenandoah National Park* two hikes have been added to bring the total to 22 circuits. The maps have been greatly improved, contours have been added, bold letters added to designate significant points on the circuit routes, and corrections made for changes that have taken place. An estimate of hiking time has been made for each hike.

In areas which may go into wilderness most of the fire roads shown on the maps will be allowed to revert to trails. It normally takes about 10 years for a well constructed and drained road to completely revert to trail status.

***Distances*** are given in the text in miles as well as kilometers. All distances are rounded off to 0.1 mi. The kilometer distance has been extended from this figure and rounded off to 0.1 km.

***Time estimates*** for the circuits are based on a hiking speed of 2 mi. (3.2 km.) per hour. This basic time has been corrected upward for elevation gain and difficulty. Using these estimates the user of this booklet should be able to select hikes to suit his available time and hiking ability.

Since these trails go through a National Park, the park regulations must be followed. Pets must be on leash, no firearms may be carried, and fires are to be made only at designated locations. Fires in backcountry are limited to self contained gas, propane, or solid fuel stoves. Camping permits are required. All camping permits are based on primitive camping and locations are assigned by the Park to the individual. No fires. No overnight camping at shelters except during periods of severely unseasonable weather. Pack out what you carry in. *Do Not Litter.*

Any questions, difficulties, or corrections related to this booklet should be brought to the attention of the Editor, care of PATC.

***Elevation Change,*** where shown, is an estimate of the

total ascent or descent on the circuit. It is not necessarily the difference in elevation between the lowest and highest points on the circuit.

## Abbreviations

| | |
|---|---|
| *AT* | Appalachian Trail |
| km | kilometers |
| mi. | miles |
| MP | mileposts on the Skyline Drive |
| *SNP* | Shenandoah National Park |

# LEGEND

## TRAIL BLAZES

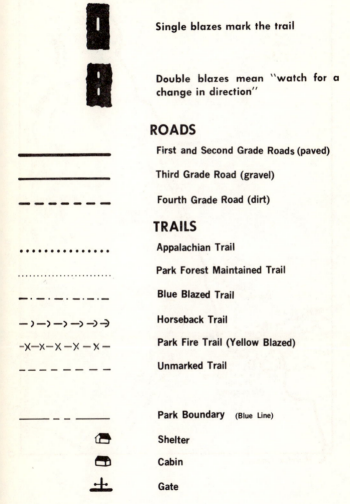

Single blazes mark the trail

Double blazes mean "watch for a change in direction"

## ROADS

— First and Second Grade Roads (paved)

— Third Grade Road (gravel)

------ Fourth Grade Road (dirt)

## TRAILS

............... Appalachian Trail

............... Park Forest Maintained Trail

-·-·-·-·-·- Blue Blazed Trail

-›-›-›-›-›-› Horseback Trail

-x-x-x-x-x- Park Fire Trail (Yellow Blazed)

------ Unmarked Trail


——  —  —  —— Park Boundary (Blue Line)

⌂ Shelter

⌂ Cabin

⊥ Gate

All maps drawn to 100 foot (30.48 meters) contour intervals.

ix

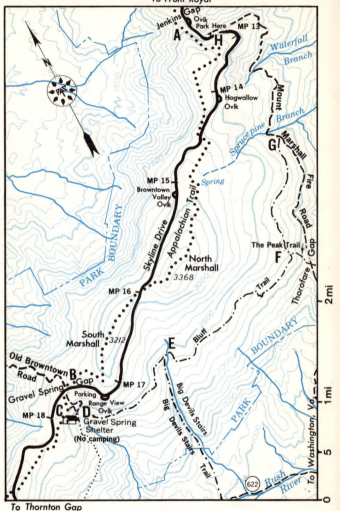

# 1 Hike No. 1
# BLUFF TRAIL

13.1 mi. (21.1 km.); 6hrs. 30 min.
*Map Direction:* (A-B-C-D-E-F-G-H-A)

The trails on this hike are in good condition and have adequate signposts. During late summer, high weeds may be encountered on the upper end of Mount Marshall Fire Road but hiking traffic usually keeps a path open through them.

The Bluff Trail is nearly level and passes through a splendid forest growth. A moderate amount of climbing is provided on the *AT* section of the hike as it climbs the peaks of North and South Marshall Mts., but it is an easy hike despite being 13 miles long. Some fine views of peaks and surrounding valleys are provided from the cliffs of North Marshall and from several lookout points on South Marshall.

The shelter and spring at Gravel Spring provide a nice luncheon spot. Camping in inclement weather only.

To start the hike, park at the Jenkins Gap Overlook (A) (between MP 12 and 13). About 50 yards north and across the Skyline Drive there is a dirt service road which leads downhill to the *AT*. Follow this road and turn left, south, on the *AT*. The distance to be hiked on the *AT* is 5.6 mi. (9.0 km.).

There is a slight upgrade and then a downgrade to take the trail across the Drive between MP 14 and 15. Then comes a steady uphill climb to the top of North Marshall (3368 ft-1027 meters). Fine views. Descend from North Marshall and cross the Drive near MP 16. Climb over South Marshall (3212 ft-981 meters), pass several lookout points, and continue descending to Gravel Spring Gap (B) (2666 ft.-813 meters) and cross the Drive (between MP 17 and 18). Follow the *AT* which keeps to the right of the dirt road. This dirt road is the service road for Gravel Spring Shelter. In 0.2 mi. (0.3 km.) turn left from the *AT* (C) and descend via a switchbacking trail to Gravel Spring (D). Gravel Spring Shelter is to the right. Camping in inclement weather only.

From Gravel Spring take the Bluff Trail (blue-blazed) which leads to the left. After 1.4 mi. (2.3 km.) the Big Devils Stairs Trail (E) (blue-blazed) goes off to the right. Continue ahead on the Bluff Trail. At 3.2 mi. (5.2 km.) from Gravel Spring, the Peak Trail (F) (also blue-blazed) goes off to the right (see map Hike No.2). Continue ahead on the Bluff Trail and reach the Mount Marshall Fire Road (G) and follow it for 2.4 mi. (3.9 km.) to the Drive (H). Turn right on the Drive to reach your car within 0.3 mi. (0.5 km.) (A).

This circuit hike can be started from any of the points where the *AT* crosses the Drive and can of course be made in either direction. The uphill climbs are less steep in the described direction. The Skyline Drive mileposts, (MP) noted in the text, will assist the hiker in locating the access points.

## 2 Hike No. 2
# BIG DEVILS STAIRS

*Short Circuits:* 8.3 mi.(13.4 km.); 4 hrs. 25 min.
*Longer Circuit:* 10.8 mi. (17.4 km.); 5 hrs. 40 min.
*Add for Peak Circuit:* 2.2 mi.(3.5 km.); 1hr. 20 min.
*Map Direction:*
  *Short Circuit:* (A-B-C-D-F-H-A)
  *Longer Circuit:* (A-B-C-D-E-F-H-A)
  *Add for Peak Circuit:* (F-G-F)

The Big Devils Stairs canyon is one of the most impressive features of the SNP. The trail is steep and very rough, over boulders and rocks, through a narrow canyon. The area through the canyon is wooded, including some large hemlocks, and is very interesting. The exact trail route in the narrow canyon varies noticeably from year to year due to water and ice erosion of the fragile rocks-mostly ancient lavas. The inexperienced hiker should not underestimate the difficulty of this section.

Actually the Big Devils Stairs portion of this circuit hike is only 2.0 mi. (3.2 km.). The rest of the circuit is mostly easy hiking through woods along a portion of the Bluff Trail and down Mount Marshall Fire Road. A slightly longer circuit and a side trip to the Peak are described.

The start of the hike is about 70 miles (113 km.) from Washington, DC. Take US 211 to Washington, VA, taking care to turn off onto Business 211 which goes into the town. Where Business 211 turns sharply to the left in town, go right for about 100 yds. (90 meters) and turn left at the first street. This street leads into Virginia Secondary Road 622 (Harris Hollow Road). Follow 622 for 2.4 mi. (3.9 km.) to route 625. Park here (or drive up 625 for approximately 0.5 mi. (0.8 km.) where there is a small parking space on the left (H). The return portion of the hiking circuit passes this point.

Begin hiking at the junction of 622 and 625 (A) by walking along 622 for another 1.4 mi. (2.3 km.) to the beginning of the Big Devils Stairs Trail (B)—marked by a sign.

Follow the Big Devils Stairs Trail (blue-blazed) up into the canyon. At the top of the canyon reach the Bluff Trail (C). Turn right onto the Bluff Trail (blue-blazed) and follow it for 1.9 mi. (3.1 km.) to the junction with The Peak Trail (D). The *short circuit* turns right here, leaving the Bluff Trail.

(A *longer circuit* can be made by staying on the Bluff Trail for another 1.3 mi. (2.1 km.) to its junction with the Mount Marshall Fire Road (E), turning right onto the fireroad and following it for 1.5 mi. (2.4 km.) to Thoroughfare Gap (F). Total longer circuit distance 10.9 mi. (17.5 km.).

The *short circuit* descends The Peak Trail (blue-blazed) for 0.3 mi. (0.5 km.) to the Mount Marshall Fire Road in Thoroughfare Gap (F). Turn right onto the fireroad.

(The Peak Trail continues across the Mount Marshall Fire Road and climbs steeply up The Peak. This trail is very rough and care has to be taken to follow the blue blazes through the rocky terrain. The Peak Trail makes an interesting loop around the summit of The Peak (G) (2925 ft.-892 meters). Part of this loop is an old logging road. Shortly after reaching the old road a blue-blazed trail comes in from the left. This is the return loop from the summit. Continue ahead on the road and at the second point where the blue-blazed trail goes left from the road, keep straight ahead for about 0.3 mi. (0.5 km.) to an excellent view from a rock outcropping. Return to the blue-blazed trail to go to the summit (G). Continue over the summit, view point to right, and descend on the return part of the loop. Very rough).

To continue the hike, follow the Mount Marshall Fire Road downhill toward the valley. Pass a chain across the road near the Park boundary, go through a gate, and shortly after turn right downhill following blue arrows along the road through private property. Come into Virginia Secondary Road 625 at a point 1.8 mi. (2.9 km.) from Thoroughfare Gap. Follow this road—which fords the stream two times—for 0.9 mi. (1.4 km.) to 622 and the end of the hike (A).

This circuit can be combined with Hike No. 1 to start from the Skyline Drive at Jenkins Gap (between MP 12 and 13) or from Gravel Spring Gap (between MP 17 and 18). Add together the extra mileage and divide by 2 to approximate the additional time in hours.

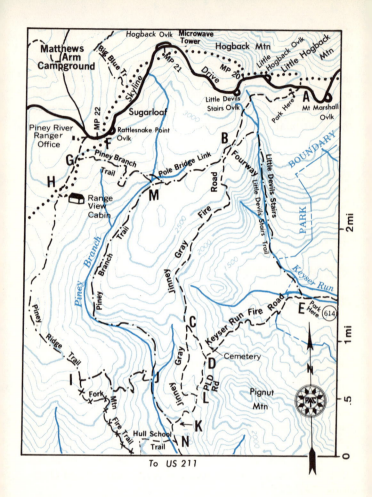

## 3 Hike No. 3
## PINEY RIDGE—LITTLE DEVILS STAIRS AREA

**I. Little Devils Stairs Circuit**
**II. Perimeter Circuit**
**III. Individual Trails**

The trails included in this grouping are in an area generally bounded by Piney Ridge, the southeastern Park boundary, Little Devils Stairs, and south of the Skyline Drive (between MP 19 and 23).

There are numerous trails in this area, which, along with fire roads, offer many potential circuit hikes. Two circuit hikes are briefly outlined and short descriptions are made of eight of these trails.

### *Highway Approaches*

The trails in this area can be approached from the Skyline Drive or from US 211-522 from points between Washington, VA, and Sperryville, VA.

***From the Skyline Drive.*** The Jinney Gray Fire Road leaves the drive between mileposts 19 and 20. The *AT* can also be reached from this point by crossing the Drive from the Jinney Gray Fire Road and following a trail for 100 yds. (90 meters) to the *AT*. Other access points to the *AT* from the Drive are at Little Hogback Overlook, Hogback Overlook and a few feet south of Rattlesnake Point Overlook (MP 22).

***From US 211-522.*** To reach the foot of Little Devils Stairs or the Keyser Run Fire Road drive on US 211-522 to the intersection of Virginia Secondary Road 622 at a point approximately 3 miles (4.8 km.) southwest of Washington, VA, or 2 miles (3.2 km.) northeast of Sperryville, VA. This intersection is at the southwest side of the highway bridge across Covington River. Follow 622 northwest toward the Park for 2.0 miles (3.2 km.) and turn left onto 614. Follow 614 for about 3 miles (4.8 km.). The last mile of this road is fairly rough. The Little Devils Stairs Trail (E) is marked by a sign and blue blazes. This is about as far as a passenger car can be driven. The road continues and in a short distance enters the Park as the Keyser Run Fire Road.

*Piney Branch.* To reach the Piney Branch area and the foot of the Jinney Gray Fire Road at (N) on the map, Piney Ridge Trail (J), and Piney Branch Trail (K), turn off US 211-522 at a point about 4 miles (6.4 km.) southwest of Washington, VA, or 1 mile (1.6 km.) northeast of Sperryville, VA and turn onto Virginia Secondary Road 612 and follow it toward the Park. 600 comes in from the left at 1.0 mile (1.6 km.). Continue ahead on 612 for 0.3 mi. (0.5 km.). Where 612 turns left continue straight ahead on 600. Follow 600 for 2.0 miles (3.2 km.) to where 653 comes in from the left, Park at or near the junction of 600-653. Use care not to block private entrances. 600 continues ahead for 0.1 mi. (0.2 km.). Hike from the end of 600, cross Piney River on a bridge and in about 0.7 mi. (1.1 km.) *ford* the river. The river is *forded twice more* inside the Park. At (N), the *second ford inside* the Park the road to the right, crossing the stream, is the Jinney Gray Fire Road. The road to the left is the Hull School Trail. The stream assumes the name Piney Branch instead of Piney River here. See map for relation of this location to other trails.


## I. Little Devils Stairs Circuit

| | | |
|---|---|---|
| Distance: | 5.7 miles | (9.2 km.) |
| Time: | 3 hrs. | 15 min. |
| Map Direction: | (E-B-C-D-E) | |

(See individual trail descriptions under III)

| Distance | Time | Map Direction |
|---|---|---|
| 2.0 mi. (3.2 km.) | Climb up Little Devils Stairs Trail to Four Way | (E-B) |
| 2.0 mi. (3.2 km.) | Turn left and descend Jinney Gray Fire Road to Keyser Run Fire Road | (B-C) |
| 1.7 mi. (2.7 km.) | Turn left and follow Keyser Run Fire Road back to start. | (C-D-E) |

This hike can be started from the Skyline Drive at (A) the beginning of the Jinney Gray Fire Road between MP 19 and 20. Hike to Four Way (B) and join the circuit there. Add 1.0 mi. (0.2 km.) for each direction for a total circuit of 7.7 miles (12.4 km.)

(A-B)
(B-A)

## II. Perimeter Circuit

| Distance | Time | Map Direction |
|---|---|---|
| 12.4 mi. (20.0 km.) | 6 hrs. 50 min | (A-F-G-H-I-J-K-L-D-E-B-A) |

(see individual trail descriptions under III)

| Distance | Trail | Map Direction |
|---|---|---|
| 0 mi. (0 km.) | Start on *AT* across from Jinney Gray Fire Road. See *AT* description. | (A) |
| 3.6 mi. (5.8 km.) | Follow *AT* south to Piney Ridge Tr. | (A-F-G-H) |
| 3.3 mi. (5.3 km.) | Descend Piney Ridge Tr. to Piney Br. Tr. | (H-I-J) |
| 0.4 mi. (0.6 km.) | Descend Piney Branch Tr. to Jinney Gray Fire Road. | (J-K) |
| 0.4 mi. (0.6 km.) | Ascend Jinney Gray Fire Road to PLD Road | (K-L) |
| 0.4 mi. (0.6 km.) | Ascend PLD Road to Keyser Run Road | (L-D) |
| 1.3 mi. (2.1 km.) | Descend Keyser Run Fire Road to the Little Devils Stairs Trail. | (D-E) |
| 2.0 mi. (3.2 km.) | Ascend the Little Devils Stairs Trail to Four Way. Turn right onto the Jinney Gray Fire Road. | (E-B) |
| 1.0 mi. (1.6 km.) | Follow the Jinney Gray Fire Road to the Skyline Drive. | (B-A) |
| 12.4 mi. (20.0 km.) | Total distance. | |

## III. Individual Trail Descriptions:

### 1. Appalachian Trail

    Direction of description—north to south
    Distance along AT:     3.6 mi.     (5.8 km.)
    Time:                  1 hr.       30 min.
    Map Direction:         (A-F-G-H)

Across the Skyline Drive from the entrance to the Jinney Gray Fire Road (A) (between MP 19 and 20) follow the spur trail and within 100 yds. (90 meters) come onto the *AT.* Turn left and follow the *AT* southward. Climb over Little Hogback Mtn. and the Hogback Mtn. and cross the Drive twice near Hogback Overlook (MP 21). After a long descent cross the Skyline Drive (F) between Rattlesnake Point Overlook and MP 22. At 0.4 mi. (0.6 km.) beyond the Drive the Piney Branch Trail (G) goes left. Continue on the *AT*, not the dirt road on the right, and in another 0.4 mi. (0.6 km.) reach the dirt road (H) again. This is the end of the portion of the *AT* used in the circuit hike. (The dirt road leads downhill to Range view cabin. Reservation through The Potomac Appalachian Trail Club.) A few feet down this road the Piney Ridge Trail goes to the right. Total distance on the *AT* 3.6 mi. (5.8 km.).

### 2. Piney Ridge Trail (blue-blazed)

    Direction of description—south then east-descending.
    Distance:              3.3 miles   (5.2 km.)
    Time:       (down)     1 hr.       40 min.
                (up)       2 hr.       0 min.
    Map Direction:         (H-I-J)

At a point on the *AT* (H) 0.8 mi. (1.3 km.) south from the *AT* crossing of the Skyline Drive near Rattlesnake Point turn left onto the Range View Cabin maintenance road. In a few feet turn right onto the Piney Ridge Trail (blue-blazed). This trail leads along Piney Ridge through a naturally reforested area which was grazing and farmland before the establishment of the Park. An old mountain cemetery is passed on the right at 2.0 miles (3.2 km.). Continue downhill and in 100 yds. (90 meters) farther the Piney Ridge Trail (I) turns sharply to the left. (The Fork Mtn. Fire Trail (yellow-blazed) goes straight ahead. Exploration only.)

After the left turn, the Piney Ridge Trail descends and meanders through a deserted homesite area and then descends along an abandoned old farm road. Reach the Piney Branch Trail (J) at 3.3 mi. (5.3 km.). This junction is 0.4 mi. (0.6 km.) from the lower end of Piney Branch Trail at the Jinney Gray Fire Road (K) or 3.8 mi. (6.1 km.) from the upper end of the Piney Branch Trail (G) at the *AT*.

### 3. Piney Branch Trail (blue-blazed)

Direction of description—generally south-descending.
Distance:          4.2 mi.      (6.8 km.)
Time:      (down)  2 hr.        10 min.
           (up)    2 hrs.       30 min.
Map Direction:     (G-M-J-K)

This trail leaves the *AT* at (G) 0.4 mi. (0.6 km.) south of the Skyline Drive crossing near Rattlesnake Point and leads 4.2 mi. (6.8 km.) down to the Jinney Gray Fire Road (K).

Descend through overgrown fields into woods. At 1.2 mi. (1.9 km.) pass a short cut (signpost) to Pole Bridge Link Trail leading to the left. Via this trail it is 1.1 mi. (1.8 km.) to Four Way at the head of the Little Devils Stairs Trail.

Continue down hill and at (M) 1.3 mi. (2.1 km.) from the *AT* pass the Pole Bridge Link Trail leading left. It is 1.0 mi. (1.6 km.) from this point to Four Way.

Continue with Piney Branch to the right deep down in the valley. Cross Piney Branch three times and reach the junction (J) with the Piney Ridge Trail at 3.8 mi. (6.1 km.). The portion of the trail along Piney Branch is rough and rocky. Cross Piney Branch again at 3.9 mi. (6.3 km.) and continue to the Jinney Gray Fire Road (K). See Jinney Gray Fire Road description.

## 4. Jinney Gray Fire Road

| Distance: | | 6.3 mi. | (10.1 km.) |
|---|---|---|---|
| Time: | (down) | 3 hrs. | 10 min. |
| | (up) | 3 hrs. | 50 min. |
| Map Direction: | | (A-B-C-L-K-N-and off the map to Va. 600) | |

This fire road, gated at the Skyline Drive and the Park boundary, makes an excellent hiking route. It is a major trunk line to connect the various trails and makes possible a number of circuit hikes. It leads from the Drive (A) between MP 19 and 20 to the Park boundary at Piney River and continues outside the park through private land to Virginia Secondary Road 600. See HIGHWAY APPROACHES-PINEY BRANCH for directions to reach 600.

Points and map references along the road are:

| Map | Mile | (km.) | | Mile | (km.) |
|---|---|---|---|---|---|
| A | 0 | 0 | Skyline Drive (between mp. 19-20) | 6.3 | (10.1) |
| B | 1.0 | (1.6) | Four Way. Pole Bridge Link Trail to right. Little Devils Stairs Trail to left | 5.3 | (8.5) |
| C | 3.0 | (4.8) | Keyser Run Road | 3.3 | (5.3) |
| L | 3.9 | (6.3) | PLD Road | 2.4 | (3.9) |
| K | 4.3 | (6.9) | Piney Branch Trail. Piney Ridge Trail is 0.4 mi. (6.4 km.) up this trail. | 2.0 | (3.2) |
| N | 4.4 | (7.1) | Ford Piney Branch, Hull School Trail goes to right. | 1.9 | (3.1) |
| off map | 6.3 | (10.1) | Virginia Secondary Road No. 600 | 0 | 0 |

## 5. Pole Bridge Link Trail (blue-blazed)

| | | |
|---|---|---|
| Direction of description—west. | | |
| Distance: | 1.0 mi. | (1.6 km.) |
| Time: | 0 hrs. | 30 min. |
| Map Direction: | (B-M) | |

This trail provides a link between the Jinney Gray Fire Road and the Piney Branch Trail. The trail starts at Four Way (B) on the Jinney Gray Fire Road and follows old roads for 0.8 mi. (1.3 km.) where it branches. The right, upper, branch reaches the Piney Branch at a point 1.1 mi. (1.9 km.) from the *AT* and the lower branch reaches the Piney Branch (M) at 1.3 mi. (2.1 km.)

## 6. Keyser Run Fire Road

| | | | |
|---|---|---|---|
| Direction of description-west-climbing. | | | |
| Distance: | | 1.7 mi. | (2.7 km.) |
| Time: | (down) | 0 hrs. | 50 min. |
| | (up) | 1 hrs. | 0 min. |
| Map Direction: | | (E-D-C) | |

This fire road is an extension of Virginia Secondary Road 614 into the Park. It is chained at the Park boundary. It affords a link between the lower end of Little Devils Stairs Trail and the Jinney Gray Fire Road at point (C) or by using the PLD road from (D) Bolen Cemetery. The Jinney Gray Road is reached at point (L).

## 7. PLD Road (*P*iney-*L*ittle *D*evils)

| | | |
|---|---|---|
| Distance: | 0.4 mi. | (0.6 km.) |
| Time: | 0 hrs. | 15 min. |
| Map Direction: | (L-D) | |

This road serves as a connecting link between Jinney Gray Fire Road and the Keyser Run Fire Road. It can be used in circuits involving trails in the Piney Branch area and Little

Devils Stairs. It connects with the Jinney Gray Fire Road at point (L) 0.4 mi. (0.6 km.) up Jinney Gray from the Piney Branch Trail and with the Keyser Run Fire Road at (D) a point on that road 1.3 mi. (1.8 km.) from the lower end of the Little Devils Stairs Trail.

### 8. Little Devils Stairs Trail (blue-blazed)

Direction of descriptions-north-ascending.
Distance:           2.0 miles      (3.2 km.)
Time:       (down)  1 hr.          10 min.
            (up)    1 hr.          30 min.
Map Direction:      (E-B)

This trail (blue-blazed) leads from (E) near the end of Virginia Secondary Road 614 to (B) Four Way at a point 1.0 mi. (1.6 km.) on the Jinney Gray Fire Road from the Skyline Drive. The trail is steep and rough, and it climbs over boulders and crosses and recrosses Keyser Run in a deep ravine. This is a rewarding hike in any season. It should not be overlooked in winter when the cascades and pools are frozen solid making a winter fairyland.

It is recommended that this trail be climbed rather than descended. The rocks can be slippery and a person is less likely to slip in climbing than in descending.

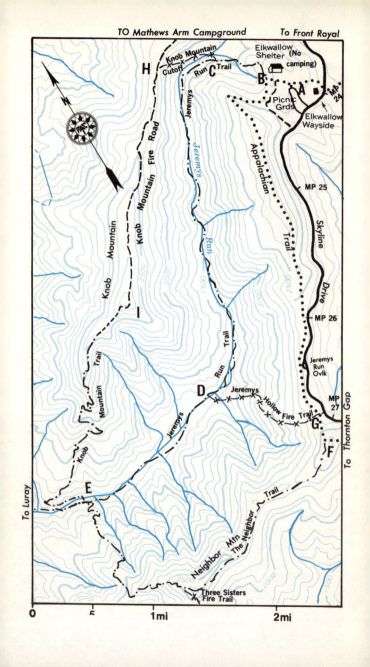

## 4 Hike No. 4
## JEREMYS RUN—NEIGHBOR TRAIL

14.0 miles (22.5 km.); 7 hrs. 40 min.
*Total elevation change:* 2600 ft. (792 meters)
*Map direction:* (A-B-C-D-E-F-G-B-A)

Jeremys Run is one of the most beautiful streams in the Northern Section of the Park, and the trail crosses it many times to make it a most interesting walk. There is considerable descent and ascent in this circuit hike. Starting at 2390 ft. (728 meters) at Elkwallow it drops to 1070 ft. (326 meters) at the foot of the Neighbor Trail and then climbs up again to 2700 ft. (323 meters) on Neighbor Mountain. Interim ups and downs along the circuit increase the elevation difference hiked to approximately 2600 ft. (792 meters).

Start the hike at the lower end of the Elkwallow picnic area (A) (entrance just south of the wayside) near MP 24. There is a parking area at the lower end of the picnic area. Take the trail leading from this parking area downhill past the comfort station and come onto the *AT* in a few feet. Continue downhill on the *AT* past the Elkwallow shelter on the right—spring on left. As with other shelters in the Park, overnight use is prohibited except in inclement weather. After 0.3 mile (0.5 km.) on the *AT* reach the Jeremys Run Trail (B)—blue blazed. Continue straight ahead downhill on the Jeremys Run Trail. (At (C) 0.8 mile (1.3 km.) from the start of the Jeremys Run Trail the Knob Mtn. Cutoff Fire Trail, marked by a concrete signpost and yellow blazes, leads to the right, crosses Jeremys Run and climbs to the Knob Mtn. Fire Road. This trail offers a means of including Knob Mtn. Trail in other circuit hikes.)

Continue down stream, crossing Jeremys Run 14 times. Pass Jeremys Hollow Fire Trail (D), yellow blazed, on the left after 3.9 miles (6.3 km.) on the Jeremys Run Trail. This fire trail leads up to the *AT* and the Skyline Drive near MP

27. (Experienced hikers only.) Continue on the blue-blazed trail and reach the intersection with the Neighbor Trail (E) at 5.1 mi. (8.2 km.) from the start of the Jeremys Run Trail. Turn left here.

(About 50 feet (15 meters) down stream from this point the Knob Mtn. Trail comes in from across the stream on the right. Via this trail it is 5.3 miles (8.5 km.) to (H) the Knob Mtn. Cutoff or 7.5 miles (12.1 km.) to Matthews Arm Campground.)

Climb up the Neighbor Trail via switchbacks. There are a few stands of white birch along this trail. The Three Sisters Fire Trail, yellow blazed, goes off to the right at 2.6 miles (4.2 km.) a short distance before the summit of The Neighbor is reached. The Three Sisters Trail leads out to private land in 1.8 mile (2.9 km.). This is for exploration only.

Follow the Neighbor Trail along the crest of Neighbor Mountain, passing over several small knobs. There are occasional wintertime views. Reach the *AT* (F) at 4.6 miles (7.4 km.) from Jeremys Run.

Turn left, downhill, and follow the *AT* northward. After 0.2 mile (0.3 km.) on the *AT* a short trail leads right (east) to the Skyline Drive near MP 27.* Continue on the *AT* and in a few yards cross the Jeremys Hollow Fire Trail (G). The *AT* continues to descend then begins a long steady climb to the high point south of Elkwallow from which it descends and after 3.7 miles (6.0 km.) on the *AT* reaches the junction with the Jeremys Run Trail (B). Turn right, uphill, and follow the *AT* and the short side trail back to the parking lot at the picnic ground.

*This hike can also be started from the Skyline Drive just north of MP 27 (G). There is a wide grassy opening on the west side of the Drive. The *AT* can be reached within a few feet by following a side trail to the west from this area.

## 5  Hike No. 5
## HAZEL COUNTRY

The trails in the Hazel Country are mostly old farming roads which have been abandoned since the Park was established. The Hazel Mtn. Fire Road still maintains the semblance of a road and serves as a connecting link to many trails.

The mountaineer has been gone from this area for over 40 years, but there is still evidence that he was here. The trails which are for the most part his old roads, a few old houses which remain standing, the lonely chimneys, old apple orchards, decaying split rail fences, crude stone fences, and overgrown fields which are now forested in pine, all remind you of the mountaineer. The observant hiker will soon realize that only the steepest slopes were forested. The rest was cultivated or in grass. The views from the high open areas must have been grand.

The multitude of trails in the area makes it beyond the scope of this guide to include descriptions of all of them. Instead, two circuits will be briefly outlined and a tabulation of trails with map references of terminal points and estimated mileages and time estimates will be made. This should aid the hiker in making up his own circuits. For detailed descriptions see "Guide to the Appalachian Trail and Side Trails in The Shenandoah National Park" published by the Potomac Appalachian Trail Club, Inc.

### *Highway Approaches*

The Hazel Country is about 80 miles (129 km.) from Washington, DC. To reach this area from the northeast, drive to Sperryville, VA, and take US 522 south for 0.8 mi. (1.3 km.) and turn onto Virginia Highway 231.

***To reach the trails leading from the Hazel Valley*** follow 231 for 3.3 mi. (5.3 km.) to the Hazel River Bridge and turn

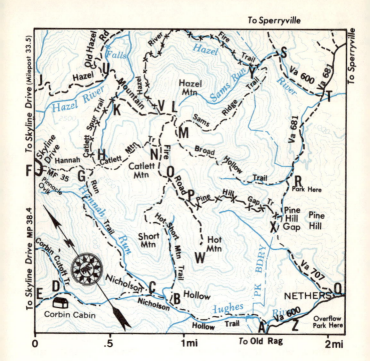

right onto 681 and follow it for about 1.0 mi. (1.6 km.) to the junction with 600 (T). This point can also be reached from Business 29 in Madison, Va. by following 231 for 17.6 mi. (28.3 km.) to 681.

***To reach the trails leading from the Hughes River Valley*** follow 231 south from its junction with 522 for 8.3 mi. (13.4 km.) and cross the Hughes River. Immediately turn west onto Virginia Secondary Road No. 602. From the other direction follow 231 for 12.7 mi. (20.4 km.) from the junction of Business 29 and 231 in Madison, Va. The road up the river changes numbers several times. It becomes 601, 707, then 600. The important thing is not to cross the Hughes River after leaving 231. At 3.5 mi. (5.6 km.), just beyond Nethers, at (Z), there is a SNP "Temporary Parking" area. Park here or continue another 0.5 mi. (0.8 km.) to the Nicholson Hollow Trail junction (A). If parking at a spot other than a parking place be sure not to leave the car on the pavement or it may be towed away.

## Circuit 1. Pine Hill Gap—Broad Hollow

5.9 mi. (9.5 km.); 3 hrs. 30 min.
*Map Direction:* (R-X-P-O-N-L-M-R)

See Highway Approaches to reach trails leading from the Hazel River Valley. Drive to Point (R) on 681 and park. This can be located by a jog in the road. The Broad Hollow Trail is marked by a concrete signpost and blue blazes. Park near here.

Start the hike by continuing on 681. At the end of state maintenance, indicated by arrow on 681 sign pointing back down the road, continue ahead on the rocky road. The footway improves in a short distance. Reach Pine Hill Gap (X) in 0.5 mi. (0.8 km.) Turn right and climb via the Pine Hill Gap Trail (yellow blazed). Reach the Hazel Mtn. Fire Road (P) after 1.6 mi. (2.6 km.) on the Pine Hill Gap Trail. Turn right and follow the Hazel Mtn. Road. Pass the Hot-Short Mtn. Trail (O) in 0.4 m. (0.6 km.) then the Catlett Mtn. Trail (N) in 0.5 mi. (0.8 km.). Continue another 0.5 mi. (0.8 km.) to reach the beginning of the Sams Ridge-Broad Hollow Trails (L) (blue-blazed). Turn right. Follow the Broad Hollow Trail past where the Sams Ridge Trail (M) turns left. The Broad Hollow Trail passes several old log cabins. This trail is generally good except for several short rough spots. Reach 681 (R) and the start of the hike in 2.4 mi. (3.9 km.) from the Hazel Mtn. Fire Road.

## Circuit II. Nicholson Hollow—Hannah Run—Catlett Mtn.—Hot-Short Mtn.

9.9 mi. (15.9 km.);5 hrs. 25 min.
*Map Direction:* (A-B-C-G-N-O-B-A)

See Highway Approaches to reach trails leading from the Hughes River Valley. Start the hike at the beginning of the Nicholson Hollow Trail (A). This Trail soon crosses Brokenback Run then the Hughes River. Both of these crossings are difficult and may require wading.

After 1.7 mi. (2.7 km.) reach the Hot-Short Mtn. Trail (B) (blue-blazed) leading right. Continue on the Nicholson Hollow Trail for another 0.2 mi. (0.3 km.) to the Hannah Run Trail (C) (blue-blazed).

Climb the Hannah Run Trail. It passes several old cabin sites. Beyond the cabin sites the trail is very steep and rough. Reach the Catlett Mtn. Trail (G) (blue-blazed) after 2.5 mi. (4.0 km.) on the Hannah Run Tr. Turn right. (The Hannah Run Trail turns left and reaches the Skyline Drive at MP 35 in 1.2 mi. (1.9 km.)). Follow the Catlett Mtn. Trail. In a few yards the Catlett Mtn. Fire Foot Trail (yellow blazed) goes straight ahead and the Catlett Mtn. Trail turns right. Follow the Catlett Mtn. Trail (blue-blazed) around Catlett Mtn. to the Hazel Mtn. Fire Road (N). Turn right.

Reach the Hot-Short Mtn. Trail (O) (blue-blazed) and turn right. Descend through an old farm and orchard area and reach the Nicholson Hollow Trail (B) in 2.2 mi. (3.5 km.). Turn left and follow the Nicholson Hollow Trail back to the start (A).

## Tabulation of Individual Trails and Points on Them

| Map | Distance | | Time | | Name of Trail | Marking |
|---|---|---|---|---|---|---|
| A-B | 1.7 | 2.7 | 0 | 50 | Nicholson Hollow | (blue-blazed) |
| A-C | 1.9 | 3.1 | 0 | 55 | Nicholson Hollow | (blue-blazed) |
| A-E | 5.8 | 9.3 | 3 | 5 | Nicholson Hollow | (blue-blazed) |
| B-O | 2.2 | 3.5 | 1 | 20 | Hot-Short Mtn. | (blue-blazed) |
| C-G | 2.5 | 4.0 | 1 | 45 | Hannah Run | (blue-blazed) |
| G-F | 1.2 | 1.9 | 0 | 45 | Hannah Run | (blue-blazed) |
| G-N | 1.2 | 1.9 | 0 | 35 | Catlett Mtn. | (blue-blazed) |
| H-K | 1.0 | 1.6 | 0 | 30 | Catlett Spur | (yellow-blazed) |
| J | 0 | | 0 | | Hazel Mtn. Fire Road | (Skyline Drive Mile 35.5) |
| J-U | 1.6 | 2.6 | 0 | 50 | Hazel Mtn. Fire Road | (none) |
| U-K | 0.6 | 1.0 | 0 | 20 | Hazel Mtn. Fire Road | (yellow post at K) |
| K-V | 0.7 | 1.1 | | 20 | Hazel Mtn. Fire Road | (yellow post at V) |
| V-L | 0.2 | 0.3 | 0 | 10 | Hazel Mtn. Fire Road | (concrete sign post at L) |
| L-N | 0.5 | 0.8 | 0 | 15 | Hazel Mtn. Fire Road | (concrete sign post at N) |
| N-O | 0.5 | 0.8 | 0 | 15 | Hazel Mtn. Fire Road | (concrete sign post at O) |
| O-P | 0.4 | 0.6 | 0 | 10 | Hazel Mtn. Fire Road | (yellow post at P) |
| P-W | 0.7 | 1.1 | 0 | 20 | Hazel Mtn. Fire Road | (end of road at W) |
| Total Length: | | | | | | |
| J-W | 5.2 | 8.3 | 2 | 40 | | |
| Y-V | 2.4 | 3.9 | 1 | 30 | Hazel River Trail | (yellow blazed) |
| S-Y | 0.4 | 0.6 | 0 | 15 | Hazel River Road | (hiking only-private) |
| L-M | 0.2 | 0.3 | 0 | 5 | Sams Ridge-Broad Hollow | (blue-blazed) |
| M-Y | 1.6 | 2.6 | 1 | 0 | Sams Ridge | (blue-blazed) |
| M-R | 2.2 | 3.5 | 1 | 25 | Broad Hollow | (blue-blazed) |
| P-X | 1.6 | 2.6 | 1 | 0 | Pine Hill Gap Trail | (yellow-blazed) |
| R-X | 0.5 | 0.8 | 0 | 15 | Virginia 681 | (not maintained all way to X) |
| Q-X | 1.4 | 2.3 | 0 | 50 | Virginia 707 | (not maintained all way to X) |

Catlett Spur and Hazel River Fire Foot Trails are for experienced hikers only.

Pine Hill Gap Trail, although in the yellow blazed category, is an old road and is easily followed.

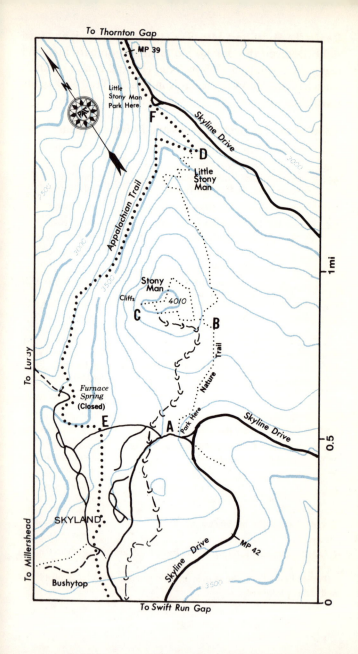

## 6 Hike No. 6
# STONY MAN MOUNTAIN

*Short Circuit:* 3.0 mi. (4.8 km.); 1 hr. 30 min.
*Longer Circuit:* 4.2 mi. (6.8 km.); 2 hrs. 5 min.
*Map Direction:* (A-B-C-B-D-E-A) (F-D-E-A-B-C-B-D-F)

This is one of the most scenic circuits in the Park. The trails are in good condition, well marked with signs, and the grades are not difficult. Stony Man Mountain is the second highest peak in the Park, 4010 ft. (1222 meters). The climb from the parking lot is only about 300 feet.

The beginning of this hike is along a Park Service Nature Trail along which the botanical and geological features are marked by appropriate signs.

The panoramic views from Stony Man, Little Stony Man and the *AT* sections of the hike are outstanding. Stony Man gets its name from its resemblance to a stone face, which can be clearly seen from the Skyline Drive as you approach from the north.

The area around Skyland and Stony Man Mtn. was developed before the Skyline Drive or Park were established. George Freeman Pollock developed the Skyland recreation area with hiking and horseback riding trails and hotel accommodations. Skyland was reached by a steep mountain road from Luray. Horse drawn wagons were used at first to carry supplies and guests. The last bit of this hike along the *AT* follows that old road.

The entrance to Skyland is marked by a sign on the right of the Drive just south of MP 41. (The sign is sometimes taken down in winter, but the hard-surfaced road is unmistakable.). Turn onto this road and park in the Nature Trail Parking lot on the right (A).

The start of the Stony Man Trail (A) is marked by a sign at the edge of the parking lot. In 0.4 mi. (0.6 km.) reach a cross trail (B). The Nature Trail goes straight ahead to the summit loop trail (C). This summit loop, 0.4 mile (0.6 km.) long, can be hiked in either direction. There are several viewpoints from the rock outcroppings. Time should be allowed for viewing from these points.

Return down to the cross trail (B). Turn left (north), and descend toward Little Stony Man Cliffs on the Little Stony Man Trail. Reach Little Stony Man at 0.8 mi. (1.3 km.) from the start of the hike. Excellent view. Continue and in 0.2 mi. (0.3 km.) reach the *AT* (D). Turn left and follow the *AT* for 1.3 mi. (2.1 km.) back to Skyland. On reaching Skyland area (E) take the first hard surfaced road to the left. This within 0.2 mi. (0.3 km.) will take you back to the parking lot (A). Circuit distance is 3.0 mi. (4.8 km.).

The longer circuit is made by starting from the Little Stony Man parking place (F), marked by a sign on the west side of the Drive just south of MP 39 and not far south from Little Stony Man Overlook. A short path from the parking place leads to the *AT*. Turn left on the *AT*. In 0.6 mi. (1.0 km.) the Little Stony Man Trail (D) comes into the *AT*. Join the circuit here. Circuit from Little Stony Man Parking is 4.2 mi. (6.8 km.).

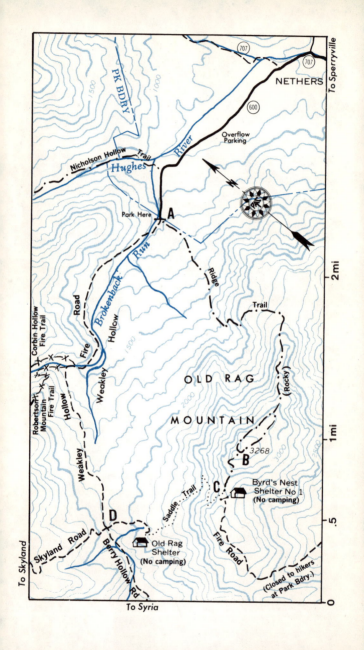

# 7 Hike No. 7
# OLD RAG MOUNTAIN

| | | |
|---|---|---|
| Distance: | 7.1 miles | (11.4 km.) |
| Time: | 5 hrs. | |
| Elevation change: | 2188 ft. | (667 meters) |
| Map Direction: | (A-B-C-D-A) | |

Old Rag Mountain, originally called "Old Raggedy" Mountain, is the most spectacular mountain in the Northern Virginia Blue Ridge. It is an outlying mountain, not part of the continuous chain. Views from the rocky ridge trail extend in all directions, including a noble panorama of the mountains in the central section of the Shenandoah National Park.

Old Rag is popular with hikers in all seasons and on weekends in Spring and Summer it is actually overcrowded. The main attraction is the rock scramble up the Ridge Trail. Also in spring the redbud dogwood, trillium and other wild flowers put on their displays.

The trails are clear and well signed. The Ridge Trail is blue-blazed from the parking lot across the summit and down to Byrd Shelter No. 1. There are several springs on the way to the top via the Ridge Trail, and another near the summit. None of them, however, can be relied on in dry weather, so it is best to carry a filled canteen.

Just below the summit is the Byrd's Nest No. 1 Shelter, built by the late Senator Harry F. Byrd, Sr. This is for overnight use *in inclement weather only*. There is no spring here. Near the base of the mountain in the saddle between Old Rag and the main Blue Ridge is the Old Rag Shelter with a spring. *Camping forbidden except in inclement weather*. These shelters and fireplaces can be used for cooking but should not be relied on because of the heavy demand for their use.

The start of the hike is 80 miles from Washington, DC Take US 522 south from Sperryville, VA. and in 0.8 mi. (1.3

km.) turn onto Virginia Highway 231. At 8.3 miles (13.4 km.) from the junction of 522-231 cross Hughes River and immediately turn right, west, onto Virginia Secondary Road No. 602. (Coming from the opposite direction it is 12.7. miles (20.4 km.) from the junction of 231 and Business 29 in Madison, VA.)

The road up the river changes numbers several times. It becomes 601, 707, then 600. The important thing is not to cross the Hughes River after leaving Va. Highway 231. At 3.5 mi. (5.6 km.), just beyond Nethers, there is a SNP "Temporary or Overflow Parking" area. Park here or continue for another 0.8 mi. (1.3 km.) to the end of 600, where there is a small parking area at the beginning of the circuit (A). This area is usually full. If parking at other than parking lots be sure your car is off the pavement or it may be towed away.

To begin the hike go to the end of 600 (A) and turn left onto the Ridge Trail (blue-blazed). After a steady climb thru woods the trail comes out into the open onto rocks. The trail climbs over, under and around large boulders, squeezes through rock slits and goes through a tunnel in the rocks. The summit (B), 3291 ft. (1003 meters), is reached after 2.7 mi. (4.3 km.). Continue following the blue blazes down to Byrd's Nest No. 1 (C). *Overnight camping in inclement weather only.* At sign post turn right and descend via the Saddle Trail. *Do not go east down closed Fire Road.*

Reach Old Rag Shelter. (Inclement weather camping only.) There are two route choices from here. Turn right and follow the dirt road, or descend to the spring in front of the Shelter and bushwhack a few feet along the spring branch to a trail below. Follow the trail. Both end at the junction of Weakley Hollow, Berry Hollow, and the Skyland—Old Rag Fire Roads (D). This point is 4.6 mi. (7.4 km.) from the beginning of the hike. Turn right onto the Weakley Hollow Fire Road and follow it 2.5 mi. (4.0 km.) back to the starting point (A).

## Hike No. 8
# 8 CEDAR RUN-WHITEOAK CANYON

*Short Circuit:* 7.7 mi. (12.4 km.); 3 hrs. 40 min.
*Longer Circuit;* 9.1 mi. (14.7 km.); 4 hrs. 35 min.
*Map Direction;* (A-B-C-D-A) (A-B-C-E-F-G-H-A)

This circuit hike goes through two of the deepest and steepest ravines in the Shenandoah National Park, with considerable elevation change from top to bottom 2046 ft. (624 meters) for the short hike and 2305 ft. (703 meters) for the long hike. Both canyons have views of waterfalls, cascades, and high cliffs. The hike goes down Cedar Run Canyon, and comes back by way of Whiteoak Canyon, covering the best section of the Whiteoak Canyon Trail.

Both hikes are of moderate length. The longer hike adds part of the Limberlost Trail and the Crescent Rock Trail plus a short segment of the *AT*.

Start at the lower Hawksbill Gap Parking Area (A) south of MP 45. Across the Drive the Cedar Run Trail leads down toward Cedar Run. It shortly crosses the Skyland-Big Meadows Horse Trail and continues downhill past the Hawksbill Gap Shelter (no overnight camping except in inclement weather). The last chance for water is at the spring here, since drinking from the streams enroute is not recommended.

Going down Cedar Run Trail you soon pick up the stream on your right. After about 1.5 mi. (2.4 km.) the trail crosses the stream and climbs up the opposite bank. To the left note the highest cascade and deepest pool of the stream, and also the Half-Mile Cliffs just above. The trail is very rough and steep here. Recent tree falls may cause minor detours.

At point marked "X" on the map be sure to cross the stream. Avoid the old trail straight ahead. The Cedar Run Trail crosses the stream and swings around the base of the ridge and into the Whiteoak Canyon and fords the river

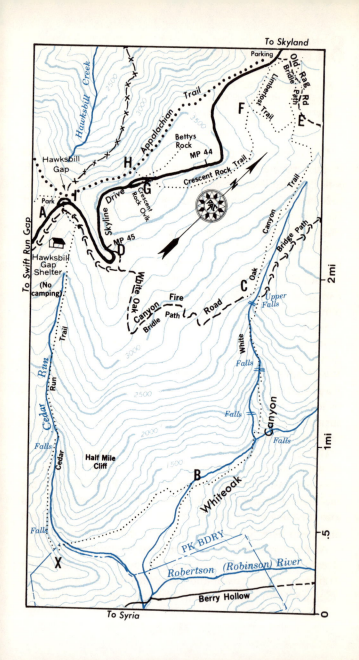

to the Whiteoak Canyon Trail (B). This point is 3.5 mi. (5.6 km.) from the start of the hike.

Go left upstream from here. Cross stream coming in from the right. The trail then begins ascending via switchbacks and passes waterfalls and cascades to the left. The cliffs on both sides of the stream are of particular interest in winter when covered with ice and icicles.

After climbing 2.1 mi. (3.4 km.) reach the Skyland-Big Meadows Horse Trail (C). Turn left and cross the stream and follow the horse trail to continue the *short circuit*. (If the water is too high to hop across, go up stream a short distance to a foot bridge, cross and come back down the other side to the horse trail).

(At this point, the *long circuit* continues on the Whiteoak Canyon trail. To do this, cross the foot bridge and turn right up stream. Reach the Limberlost Trail (E) in another 1.4 mile (2.3 km.). Signpost. Turn left and follow the Limberlost Trail for 0.4 mi. (0.6 km.) to the Crescent Rock Trail (F). Turn left and follow the Crescent Rock Trail for 1.1 mi. (1.8 km.) to the Skyline Drive (G) at Crescent Rock Overlook. Cross the Drive and follow the entrance road downhill to the parking area. At the parking area take the Betty's Rock Trail a few feet north and turn left and descend a short distance to the *AT* (H). Turn left and reach a cross trail in 0.4 mi. (0.6 km.). Turn left, uphill, to starting point (A) in Hawksbill Gap.

To continue on the *short circuit* follow the horse trail after crossing the whiteoak stream. The horse trail is marked by mileposts every 0.5 mi. (0.8 km.) Within 0.3 mi. (0.5 km.) from the stream crossing reach the 3.0 mi. (4.8 km.) milepost. This indicates the horse trail distance from the Skyline Stables. At 0.2 mi. (0.3 km.) past the 4.0 mi. (6.4 km.) milepost the horse trail turns left. There is a choice here of following the horse trail which reaches the Cedar Run Trail in 0.6 mi. (1.0 km.) in HawksbillGap (A) or staying on the dirt road which reaches the Skyline Drive in 0.1

**mi. (0.2 km.). Turn left, south, and follow the Drive for about 0.6 mi. (1.0 km.) to Hawksbill Gap (A).**

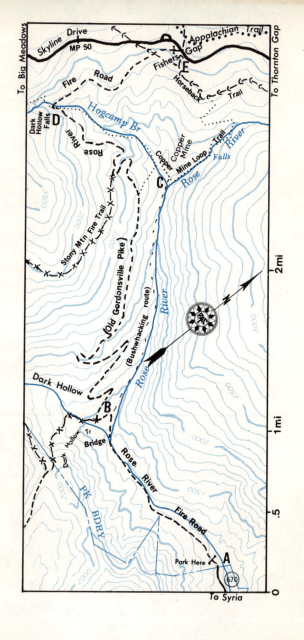

# 9 Hike No. 9
## ROSE RIVER

*Short Circuit;* 8.7 mi. (14.0 km.); 5 hrs. even.
*Longer Circuit;* 10.3 mi. (16.6 km.); 5 hrs. 50 min.
*Map Direction:* (A-B-C-D-B-A) (A-B-C-E-D-B-A)

This hike goes up the Rose River Valley on the eastern slope of the central section of the Shenandoah National Park, with the return trip all downhill along the abandoned and historic Gordonsville Pike that in pre-Park days was an important route across the mountains. It is closed to vehicle traffic and gated at the Skyline Drive and at its lower end at the Park boundary.

This hike's main attractions are the bushwhacking along Rose River for about 1.6 miles (2.6 km.) and a short side trip to Dark Hollow Falls. Rose River is a good size stream which tumbles over ledges and boulders. Falls, cascades, and pools are found along the route. The amount of water in the stream will determine the exact route along the bushwhacking portion. With low water, travel close to the stream will be best. With normal or high water the hiker will have to seek the best route along the bank or benches above the stream. This bushwhacking is not difficult but the novice should not expect a trail—he has to select his own way. Persons carrying heavy backpacks should expect this portion to be rather strenuous.

The start of this hike is about 95 miles from Washington, DC. Take US 211 to Sperryville, VA, then US 522 south for 0.8 mile (1.3 km.) and turn onto Virginia Highway 231. Follow 231 for 10 miles (16.1 km.) to Etlan, VA, and turn right onto Virginia Secondary Road No. 643 for 6 miles (9.7 km.) to Syria, VA, Turn right onto 670. This point can also be reached from Business 29 in Madison, VA, by following 231 northward 5.2 miles (8.4 km.) to the village of Banco, and in a short distance more turn left onto 670. Follow 670 thru Syria.

Beyond Syria, continue on 670, being careful to *avoid* turning onto 648. 670 continues 1.6 mile (2.6 km.) beyond the junction with 648 and ends at the Park boundary (A). There is space for several cars here. If full there is parking space back down the road opposite a white house.

From the parked car, hike up the road and into the Park. The river is on the right down in its gorge. In 1.1 mile (1.8 km.) cross a bridge over Dark Hollow Creek. In 0.1 mile (0.2 km.) beyond this bridge the road turns sharply to the left away from the river. *At this point,* (B) *leave the road* and begin following a trailless route with the river on the right. (If you should pass this turn in the road, you will reach in a short distance, a sharp turn to the right where a yellow post marks the Upper Dark Hollow Trail. If this point is reached you have gone too far. Retrace your steps to the lower bend in the road.

After about 1.4 mile (2.3 km.) of bushwhacking the river forks. Hogcamp Branch comes in from the left, Rose River from the right. Intersect the Copper Mine Trail (C) in about 0.2 mile (0.3 km.) above the fork, regardless of which side of Hogcamp Branch you happen to be on. Turn left on the Copper Mine Trail. Where the Copper Mine Trail crosses a stream (Hogcamp Branch) there is a signpost indicating trail distances along the Copper Mine Trail. A connecting trail to the Gordonsville Pike (Rose River Fireroad) leads left from this signpost. Use of this trail will shorten the loop by 1.8 miles (2.9 km.). This is not part of the circuit.

(Those wishing to add 1.6 miles (2.6 km.) to their hike can turn right on the Copper Mine Trail and follow it past Rose River Falls to reach the Gordonsville Pike in Fishers Gap (E). Turn left onto this road and rejoin the circuit at the foot of Dark Hollow Falls.)

The regular circuit continues up the Copper Mine Trail and reaches the Gordonsville Pike (Rose River Fireroad) (D) in 1.0 mi. (1.6 km.). To see Dark Hollow Falls, go right across the bridge and take the trail uphill to the left for about 200 yards (180 meters).

The rest of the trip is a stroll down the Gordonsville Pike (Rose River Fireroad). In 0.8 mi. (1.3 km.) the Stony Mtn. Fire Trail leads to the right, marked by a yellow post. This trail leads to the Rapidan Road.

In 0.4 mile (0.6 km.) farther the connecting trail from the Copper Mine Trail comes in from the left, marked by a concrete post. Continue descending and reach the Park boundary (A) in 3.7 miles (6.0 km.) more.

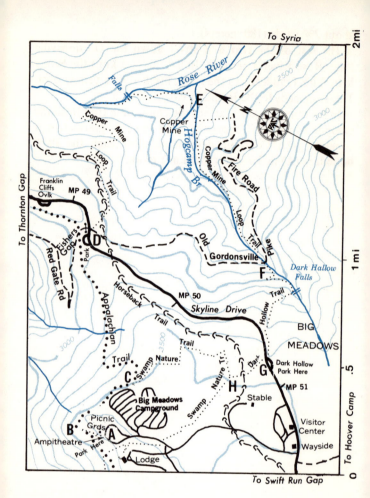

# 10 Hike No. 10
# DARK HOLLOW

*Long Circuit;* 6.0 mi. (9.7 km.); 3 hrs. even.
*Shorter Circuit;* 3.7 mi. (6.0 km.); 1 hr. 50 min.
*Map Direction;* (A-B-C-D-E-F-G-H-A) (D-F-E-D)

This is an interesting hike in which both long and short circuits pass the Rose River Falls and Dark Hollow Falls. It also passes the site of an old copper mine. There are several sites of old copper mines within the bounds of the Park but this is the only one designated. Most of the trip is wooded with few distant views except from the *AT* as it circles Big Meadows picnic and camping areas. A portion of the circuit uses part of the Swamp Nature Trail. The swamp is of interest to both amateur and professional botanists.

To reach the beginning of this circuit, drive to Big Meadows, just south of MP 51, turn in and continue to the "Amphitheatre and Swamp Nature Trail Parking" area.

Start hiking at the northeast corner of the parking space (A) and follow the Swamp Nature Trail. It leads to the *AT* (B) in a few feet. Turn right. The *AT* and Swamp Nature Trail are concurrent here. At 0.6 miles (1.0 km.), the Swamp Nature Trail (C) goes to the right and the *AT* goes to the left. Follow the *AT*.

After 1.6 miles (2.6 km.) reach Fishers Gap (D). Turn right, leaving the *AT*, and, following the road, cross the Skyline Drive, and turn left from the road onto the Copper Mine Trail. Follow the Copper Mine Loop Trail downhill. The Rose River will be on the left after several turns. Be on the lookout for Rose River Falls.

Continue down stream. The trail will swing away from the river and pass the site of a copper mine on the right of the trail. Cross a small branch then cross Hogcamp Branch. Turn right at trail junction and signpost just across Hogcamp Branch (E). Follow the Copper Mine Trail with stream on right.

Reach the Gordonsville Pike (Rose River Fireroad) (F), turn right and cross the bridge. On the opposite side of the bridge, leave the road and take the Dark Hollow Falls Trail to the left. Climb steeply past the Dark Hollow Falls. Reach the Skyline Drive (G) (Dark Hollow Parking Area on the left) and go across the Drive. Continue on the trail, cross the "Skyland-Big Meadows Horse Trail" and at 5.3 mi. (8.5 km.) from the start of the circuit reach the end of the Dark Hollow Trail (H). The Swamp Nature Trail comes in from the right. Go straight ahead and follow the nature trail. The trail crosses the entrance road to the picnic and camping areas and in a few feet reaches the end of the Swamp Nature Trail. From here the path is paved. Follow signs to the Amphitheatre and Swamp Nature Trail Parking Area (A).

For the *shorter circuit* of 3.7 mi. (6.0 km.) start at Fishers Gap (D) (south of MP 49) and go down the Gordonsville Pike. (Rose River Fire Road). At 1.0 mi. (1.6 km.) at the bridge (F) the Dark Hollow Falls Trail enters from the right. A short trip can be taken uphill on this trail for a view of the falls.

To continue the hike, cross the bridge, and immediately turn left and follow the Copper Mine Trail (E). Follow this trail past the copper mine and Rose River Falls, and continue to Fishers Gap (D).

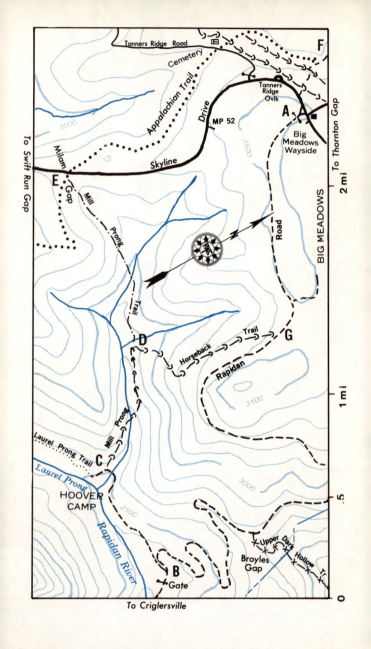

# 11 Hike No. 11
# HOOVER CAMP

9.9 mi. (15.9 km.); 5 hrs. even.
*Map Direction;* (A-G-B-C-D-E-F-A)

Hoover Camp was the Rapidan River Camp used by President Herbert Hoover as a summer fishing camp. Here he and Great Britain's Ramsey MacDonald held meetings on world armaments in 1929.

Hoover's old lodge has been kept in good condition. The lodge is beautifully located at the junction of two streams that form the Rapidan River. At the present, hiking or horseback riding are the main means of reaching the camp. The road is good from Big Meadows down to the camp but this is chained. The road from the valley is very rough and almost impassable to passenger automobiles. It is chained about a mile below the camp.

This circuit hike is an easy one. Views from the Rapidan Road are particularly good in wintertime. The hiker should walk around the Hoover Camp grounds and read signs which contain much interesting history. The climb from the camp passes a small waterfall and leads up into overgrown fields and an abandoned orchard in Milam's Gap.

To begin the hike, park at the Big Meadows Wayside just south of MP 51. Hike across the Drive to the Rapidan Road, (A) which is diagonally across from the entrance to Big Meadows (parking here beside the road also).

Hike along the road through the meadows. Deer are occasionally seen grazing in the meadows. At the far side of the meadows the road enters the woods. After 1.2 mi. (1.9 km.) the horse trail (G) turns right and leads 1.8 mi. (2.9 km.) down to Hoover camp. A shorter trip to the camp can be made by using this trail.

The circuit hike continues on the road. The road descends via switchbacks to the Rapidan River Valley. There are occasional glimpses of Fork Mtn., Doubletop Mtn., Old Rag Mtn., and the Rapidan River Valley.

After 5.4 miles (8.7 km.) a gravel road comes in downhill from the right (B). Turn onto this road and follow it uphill for 0.7 mile (1.1 km.). Cross the bridge across Mill Prong stream. On the opposite side of the bridge the Mill Prong Trail goes right. This is the beginning of the return route. To reach Hoover Camp (C) continue a few yards on the road. Before reaching the camp the Laurel Prong Trail goes off to the right.

To continue the circuit return to the Mill Prong Spur and follow it along the stream. Pass a small waterfall and in 0.8 mi. (1.3 km.) from Hoover Camp the Mill Prong Trail (D) goes straight ahead and the Mill Prong Spur Trail turns right. Go straight ahead on the Mill Prong Trail (blue-blazed). Cross two small streams and climb into overgrown fields and an abandoned orchard. Reach the *AT* (E) in Milams Gap at 1.8 mi. (2.9 km.) from Hoover Camp. Follow the *AT* across the drive. Cross Tanners Ridge Fire Road and pass a cemetery on the far side. Reach the junction of the access road to Lewis Spring shelter (F) at 1.7 mi. (2.7 km.) from Milams Gap. Turn right from the *AT* and climb the dirt road back to the Skyline Drive. Follow the drive to the left (north) to parking place.

To lengthen the hike, leave Hoover Camp (C) via the Laurel Prong Trail. Follow it to Laurel Gap 1.8 mi. (2.9 km.) and then another 1.0 mi. (1.6 km.) to the *AT* just north of Bootens Gap. Turn right onto the *AT* and follow it to Milams Gap and continue from there as in the described circuit. Total distance 13.0 mi. (20.9 km.). Time 6 hrs. 30 min. *This additional length is not shown on the map in this book.* See PATC Map No. 10.

(See note, bottom of page 51.)

# 12 *Hike No. 12* **LEWIS FALLS**

4.0 mi. (6.4 km.); 2 hrs. even.
*Map Direction:* (A-B-C-D-B-A)


Lewis Spring Falls is one of many waterfalls in the Park. Its main source of water is Lewis Spring, a large spring just below the *AT* in the hollow. The falls are reached by an interesting trail which winds down a rocky hillside. The circuit hike uses the Lewis Spring Falls Trail, a portion of the *AT*, and the access road to Lewis Spring Shelter.

To begin the hike, drive to Big Meadows Wayside, just past MP 51, and park. Walk down the Skyline Drive (south) for 0.1 mi. (0.2 km.) to a dirt road (A) going right. Follow this road downhill for about 0.3 mi. (0.5 km.) to the *AT* (B). Continue downhill.

The trail to the Falls passes to the left of the shelter–*it is not* the continuation of the road behind the shelter. Descend and reach the spur trail (C) which goes left to the falls. Reach the top of the falls within 250 ft. To get to the base of the falls, follow the trail (signpost) which descends the cliff via switchbacks. Reach the base of the falls in 0.2 mi. (0.3 km.) from their top.

To continue the hike, climb back to the Lewis Spring Falls Trail and turn left. In 1.2 mi. (1.9 km.) reach the *AT* (D). There is a choice of routes here. Turn right onto the *AT* and follow it to Lewis Spring or go by way of Black Rock. The Black Rock route rejoins the *AT* in about 0.4 mi. (0.6 km.).

(To go by Black Rock, continue straight ahead across the *AT* and take the right fork at all intersections. Pass in front of Big Meadows Lodge and follow the paved path beside the road. The way to Black Rock is indicated by signs. Reach Black Rock within 0.3 mi. (0.5 km.) from the *AT*. Excellent view. Continue across Black Rock and descend. In

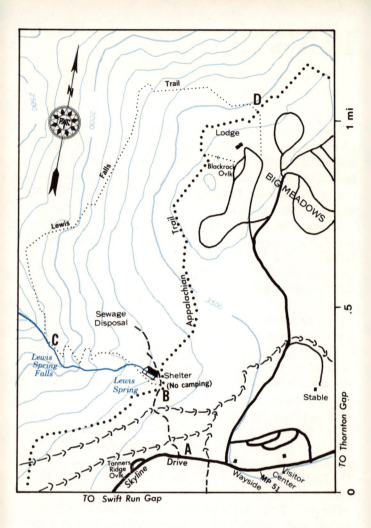

0.1 mi. (0.2 km.) reach the *AT*. Turn left, south, and continue on the circuit).

Reach the Lewis Spring Shelter access road (B) in 0.9 mi. (1.4 km.). Turn left, uphill, and climb back to the Skyline Drive and the starting point (A).

*Note:* during final stages of preparation of this booklet for printing, the possibility of Lewis Spring Shelter being torn down sometime before January 1, 1977 became known. This action was to be performed by the Park Service to prevent possibility of water contamination to Big Meadows supplies. Readers should be cautioned to note this with regard to any references to Lewis Spring Shelter in the previously described text. Depending on when you read this, *Lewis Spring Shelter may no longer exist!*

# 13 Hike No. 13
# SOUTH RIVER FALLS

*Short Circuit:* 4.3 mi. (6.9 km.); 2 hrs. 30 min.
*Long Circuit:* 9.8 mi. (15.8 km.); 5 hrs. even.
*Map Direction:* (A-B-C-B-D-E-A) (F-G-H-D-B-C-B-A-E-F)

The South River Falls is an interesting waterfall consisting of an upper and a lower cascade. The total drop is 70 ft. (21 meters) from the encircling rim of rock.

Two circuits are described. One of 4.3 mi. (6.9 km.) and one of 9.8 mi. (15.8 km.).

**The Shorter Circuit** starts at the South River Picnic Grounds (A) (between MP 62 and 63). Drive to the east end of the picnic grounds and find a sign indicating the South River Falls Trail. Park here. Hike down the trail and cross the *AT* in a few feet. You return to this point by a different route. Continue downhill and reach the top of the falls. The Park has attempted to block the paths and trails leading to the edge of the fall. The drop is about 70 feet and is very dangerous. Continue on the regular trail and come to a viewpoint at 1.0 mi. (1.6 km.). Continue on the trail and come to a dirt road (B) in 0.2 mi. (0.3 km.). To reach the base of the fall turn right and follow this road for 0.6 mi. (1.0 km.). At the end of the road find a trail (rough footway) which leads 450 ft. (137 meters) to the base of the falls (C). To return, go back up the road and continue past the Falls Trail. At 0.4 mi. (0.6 km.) past the Falls Trail the South River Fire Road (D) is intersected. Turn left and climb. Reach the *AT* (E) after 0.8 mi. (1.3 km.) on the fireroad. Turn left and follow the *AT* for 0.5 mi. (0.8 km.) to the Falls Trail. Turn right and climb to the picnic grounds. (A).

**The Longer Circuit** starts at the Pocosin Cabin Parking area (F), a short distance down the Pocosin Fire Road. Leave the Skyline Drive between MP 59 and 60. This entrance is not signed and is somewhat obscure. Do not drive past the parking space.

Hike down the fire road, pass a chain across the road, and then cross the *AT* in 0.1 mi. (0.2 km.). In a short distance pass Pocosin Cabin (locked) on the right. (Advance reservations through the Potomac Appalachian Trail Club.)

In gap at 1.0 mi. (1.6 km.) turn right onto the horse trail (signpost) (G). The ruins of the Upper Pocosin Mission are to the left of the horse trail in a few feet. A small cemetery with field stone headstones is barely recognizable on the right. The horse trail follows an old road. The road has for most of the way deteriorated to the status of trail. After about 1.2 mi. (1.9 km.) the trail enters an abandoned apple orchard. In a flat grassy area look for a turn to the right. Straight ahead leads to the South River Cemetery. A short distance after the right turn come into the South River Fire Road (H) at 1.3 mi. (2.1 km.) from the Pocosin Fire Road. Turn right and follow this road for 1.2 mi. (1.9 km.) to the junction with a road leading left downhill (D) (signpost). Turn left and descend. In 0.4 mi. (0.6 km.) the South River Falls Trail (B) turns right. To reach the base of the falls continue down the road. In 0.6 mi. (1.0 km.) reach the end of the road (C). Find a rough trail leading upstream to the base of the falls in 450 ft. (137 meters).

To continue the circuit, climb back to the Falls Trail (B) turn left, and follow it past the head of the falls and continue to the *AT* (A) in 1.2 mi. (1.9 km.). Turn right (north) on the *AT*. (For water, not in winter, go up to the picnic ground). Follow the *AT* for 3.3 mi. (5.3 km.) to the Pocosin Fire Road and the parking area (F).

# 14 Hike No. 14
# ROCKY MOUNT

9.8 mi. (15.8 km.); 5 hrs. 15 min.
*Map Direction:* (A-B-C-D-E-B-A)

This is a wild rugged area. The view from Rocky Mount across the Two Mile Run Valley is particularly impressive. The three trails used in this circuit are all blue-blazed. The circuit uses the Rocky Mount Trail, the old Gap Run Road (deteriorated to trail), and the Gap Run Trail. The descent from the summit of Rocky Mount to the Gap Run Road is rocky and rough. The total elevation change on the circuit is about 2580 ft. (786 meters).

The Rocky Mount Trail starts between mileposts 76 and the Two Mile Run Overlook (A). The Overlook is close enough to use for parking.

The trail follows a narrow ridge for most of the way to Rocky Mount. At 2.2 mi. (3.5 km.) in a ravine the Gap Run Trail goes off to the right (B). The return route comes in here.

Continue ahead and climb to the top of Rocky Mount (C) 3.4 mi. (5.5 km.) from the Drive. The cliffs just beyond the summit offer good views. Descend. Reach Gap Run Road (D) after a 2.0 mi. (3.2 km.) descent. Turn right and follow the Gap Run Road. In 0.2 mi. (0.3 km.) pass the Beldor Ridge Fire Trail leading left (yellow-blazed).

After 0.7 mi. (1.1 km.) on the Gap Run Road the Gap Run Trail goes right (E). Turn right and follow the Gap Run Trail for 1.5 mi. (2.4 km.) to the Rocky Mount Trail (B). Turn left onto the Rocky Mount Trail and follow it back to the Skyline Drive (A).

**A Longer Circuit,** *not shown* in its entirety *on the map in this book,* can be made by staying on the Gap Run Road from its junction with the Gap Run Trail (E) to the Virginia Secondary Road 628 (F). Turn right (south) on 628 and follow it into the Park and continue on the fireroad to Simmons Gap. The distance to Simmons Gap is estimated to be 3.5 mi. (5.6 km.) Follow the *AT* to the right (south) for 1.9 mi. (3.1 km.) to Pinefield Gap. Cross the Drive and continue beyond Pinefield for 0.8 mi. (1.3 km.) to where the *AT* takes a sharp turn to the left (G). Take a vague trail, about 100 ft., to the Drive just south of Two Mile Run Overlook. Total Distance 12.8 mi. (20.6 km.), 6 hrs. 20 min. See PATC Map No. 11.

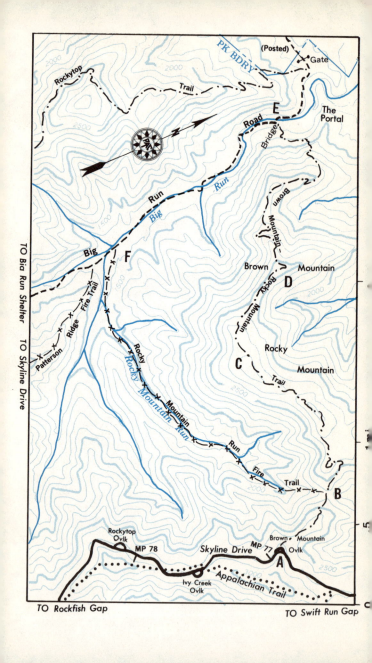

# 15 Hike No. 15
# ROCKY MOUNTAIN-BROWN MOUNTAIN

9.8 mi. (15.8 km.); 5 hrs. 10 min.
*Map Direction:* (A-B-C-D-E-F-B-A)

The hiker who has only a one-time experience in this area may be forever confused by the names of the various mountains using the word Rocky or Rock. The namers were obviously impressed with the cliffs, rock slides, and rock streams when they named Rocky Mtn., Rocky Mount, Rockytop, Rocks Mtn. and Black Rock Mtn. The names *do* convey the proper picture of the ruggedness of the area.

This circuit takes the hiker over the Rocky Mtn.-Brown Mtn. ridge down into the Big Run Valley. It follows the Big Run Fire Road upstream for 1.4 mi. (2.3 km.) to the Rocky Mtn. Run Trail. This fire foot trail, vague in spots, is followed back up the mountain.

To begin the hike, park at the Brown Mtn. Overlook (A) on the Skyline Drive just north of MP 77. Carry a filled canteen or chemical tablets to purify water from unprotected streams. The trail goes through an opening in the retaining wall at the overlook (signpost) and descends to a gap (B) in 0.7 mi. (1.1 km.). The Rocky Mtn. Run Fire Trail (yellow blazed) comes in from the left in this gap. The circuit returns to this point.

Continue ahead and climb Rocky Mountain (C). The trail is rough and rocky. For views take short detours to rock outcroppings. The route descends slightly then climbs Brown Mtn. (D), then begins a long descent which ends at Big Run Fire Road (E) in 5.3 mi. (8.5 km.) from the start. Turn left onto the fireroad. To the right, across the bridge, the Rockytop Trail comes into the fireroad in 0.5 mi. (0.8 km.). Downstream from the bridge Big Run passes through a narrow gorge known as The Portal.

Proceed up the Big Run Fire Road along the Big Run

stream. After four fords, which have to be waded except in dry weather, the Rocky Mtn. Run Trail (F) (yellow-blazed) comes in from the left. Turn onto this trail and follow it along Rocky Mtn. Run. There are several fords on this stream which have to be waded when the water is high. Near the upper end of this trail are several switchbacks. The route may be obscure here, but if the route is lost, continue up the ravine and come into the Rocky Mountain-Brown Mtn. Trail (B). Turn right, uphill, and climb 0.7 mi. (1.1 km.) back to the overlook (A).

# 16 Hike No. 16
## BIG RUN TRAIL

*Short Circuit:* 5.8 mi. (9.3 km.); 3 hrs. 5 min.
*Longer Circuit:* 6.9 mi. (1.1 km.); 3 hrs. 40 min.
*Longest Circuit:* 7.2 mi. (11.6 km.); 4 hrs. 0 min.
*Map Direction:* (A-B-C-D-A) (A-B-C-E-F-D-A) (A-B-C-E-F see text)

This circuit descends for 1140 ft. (347 meters) from the Big Run Overlook into the upper end of Big Run Valley at Big Run Shelter. It climbs out onto the ridge that forms the western side of the Big Run watershed. It joins the *AT* and parallels the Skyline Drive back to the starting point. Two slightly longer circuits are described.

The circuit starts at Big Run Overlook (A) just south of MP 81. Descend for 2.2 mi. (3.5 km.) to the Big Run Shelter (B). (Overnight use in inclement weather only.) Pass in front of the shelter and proceed a few yards down the Big Run Fire Road. Turn left onto trail (signpost) and climb 1.3 mi. (2.1 km.) to a gap at the intersection of Rocky Top Trail (C), Big Run Fire Trail, and the Big Run Trail. Turn left and continue to follow the Big Run Trail. Reach the *AT* (D) in 0.7 mi. (1.1 km.). Turn left (north) on the *AT* and follow it for 1.6 mi. (2.6 km.) to the Falls Trail (A). Turn left, uphill, and in a few feet cross the Skyline Drive to the Big Run Overlook.

**The Longer Circuit** can be made by taking the Big Run Fire Trail (yellow blazed) from its intersection with the Big Run Trail (C), descending on it for 0.3 mi. (0.5 km.) to the Madison Run Fire Road (E). Turn left, uphill, and follow the road to Browns Gap (F) in 0.8 mi. (1.3 km.). Turn left, north, onto the *AT* and follow it 0.6 mi. (1.0 km.) to its junction with the east end of Big Run Trail (D). Rejoin the shorter circuit and continue on the *AT* for another 1.6 mi. (2.6 km.) to the beginning of the circuit (A).

The *longest circuit* is made by following the longer hike as described above to (F) Browns Gap, cross the Skyline

Drive and follow the Browns Gap Fire Road (goes off the map) for 1.7 mi. (2.7 km.) to the Falls Trail (marked by a signpost). Turn left, uphill, onto the Falls Trail and follow it for 0.9 mi. (1.4 km.) back to the Skyline Drive Overlook (A).

*Note:* Parking areas at Big Run Overlook (A) are usually full. For the two shortest circuits, parking is available at Doyle River Overlook just north of MP 82. The *AT* passes through this overlook. Hike north from here to (A). Browns Gap (F), just north of MP 83, affords some parking for hikers following the two longer circuits.

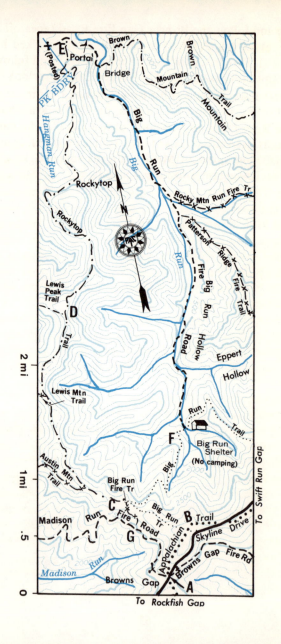

# 17 Hike No. 17
# ROCKYTOP

14.6 mi. (23.5 km.); 7 hrs. 20 min.
*Map Direction:* (A-B-C-D-E-F-C-B-A) or -C-G-A)

The Rocky Top Ridge forms the west side of Big Run Valley. It extends northward from the high point about 0.6 mi. (0.8 km.) north of Browns Gap (MP 83) for about 6 miles to where the Big Run cuts through a narrow gorge called The Portal. Three major ridges extend westward from the Rockytop Ridge. These ridges terminate in peaks, Austin Mtn., Lewis Mtn., and Lewis Peak. These peaks and the deep stream valleys make rugged scenery in winter. Summer foliage blocks the views except in the most exposed places. The hiker should note the fossilized worm holes to be found in some of the rock. Look for them where the trail crosses rock slides.

The circuit route drops from 2860 ft. (871 meters) down to 1240 ft. (378 meters) for an elevation difference of 1620 ft. (494 meters). The many ups and downs on Rockytop ridge bring the total vertical difference to approx. 2440 ft. (744 meters).

The hike starts at Browns Gap (A) just north of MP 83. Hike north on the *AT* for 0.6 mi. (1.0 km.) and turn left onto the Big Run Trail (B). Reach the beginning of the Rockytop Trail (C) after 0.7 mi. (1.1 km.) on the Big Run Trail. The Big Run Trail goes right and the Big Run Fire Trail (yellow blazed) goes left. Continue ahead across the gap on the Rockytop Trail (blue-blazed). Pass the Austin Mountain Trail (yellow-blazed) to the left at 0.4 mi. (0.6 km.), the Lewis Mountain Trail (yellow-blazed) to the left at 1.3 mi. (2.1 km.), and the Lewis Peak Trail (D) (blue-blazed) at 2.2 mi. (3.5 km.).

Reach the Big Run Fire Road (E) after 5.7 mi. (9.2 km.) on the Rockytop Trail. Turn right.

In 0.5 mi. (0.8 km.) the road crosses Big Run on a bridge. The Rocky Mountain-Brown Mountain Trail comes in from the left just across the bridge. Continue on the road. In 1.4 mi. (2.3 km.) from the bridge and after fording Big Run four times, the Rocky Mountain Run Fire Trail (yellow blazed) comes in from the left. *Cross* Rocky Mtn. Run and in 0.2 mi. (0.3 km.) more the Patterson Ridge Fire Trail (yellow-blazed) comes in from the left. Reach the Big Run Trail (F) after 5.0 mi. (8.1 km.) on the Big Run Fire Road. The Big Run Shelter is on the left (camping in inclement weather only.) Turn right (west) onto the Big Run Trail (signpost) and climb to the Rockytop Ridge (C) in 1.3 mi. (2.1 km.). Turn left and follow the Big Run Trail (B) and the *AT* back to Browns Gap (A).

(Browns Gap can also be reached by following The Big Run Fire Trail (yellow-blazed) for 0.3 mi. (0.5 km.) down to the Madison Run Fire Road (G). Follow it to the left, uphill, for 0.8 mi. (1.3 km.) to Browns Gap (A). This alternate route is 0.2 mi. (0.3 km.) shorter than the other route.)

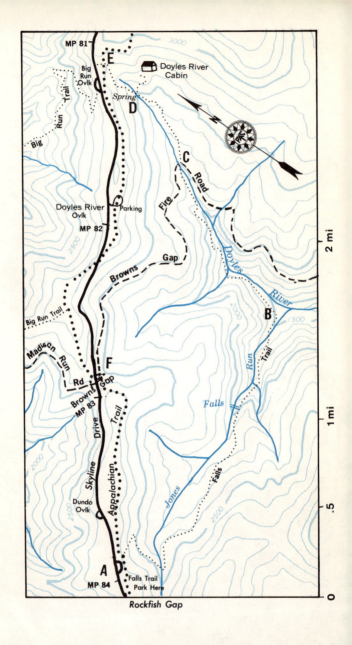

# 18 Hike No. 18
# FALLS TRAIL

*Short Circuit:* 6.5 mi. (10.5 km.); 3 hrs. 15 min.
*Long Circuit:* 7.9 mi. (12.7 km.); 4 hrs. 0 min.
*Map Direction:* (A-B-C-F-A) (A-B-C-D-E-F-A)

This is an interesting circuit. It descends the Jones Falls Run Trail down past the Jones Falls Run waterfall to Doyle River. It descends 1330 ft. (405 meters) before beginning its climb up Doyle River. The trail up Doyle River is rather steep and narrow where it climbs past the lower fall. The upper fall is situated in a grove of mature hemlock. At the Browns Gap Fire Road (C), a short circuit of 6.5 mi. (10.5 km.) can be made by using this road and the *AT* to return to the parking place. The long hike continues on the Falls Trail to the *AT* and follows the *AT* back to the parking place.

To begin the hike park at the Falls Parking Area (A) a few feet north of milepost 84. Follow the Falls Trail, cross the *AT*, and continue downhill. It soon passes a fairly high waterfall, 42 ft. (12.8 meters), then several smaller ones. Near the junction of Jones Falls Run and the Doyle River (B) the trail swings left and climbs along the Doyle River. It climbs via switchbacks past the lower fall, 63 ft. (19.2 meters), and in a short distance comes to the upper fall.

Continue climbing and come to the Browns Gap Fire Road (C) at 3.7 mi. (6.0 km.). Here the *shorter circuit* turns left and climbs by an easy grade to Browns Gap (F). In Browns Gap go left, do not cross the drive, and follow the *AT* south for 1.1 mi. (1.8 km.) to the Falls Trail parking area (A).

*The Longer Circuit* continues across the Browns Gap Fire Road (C) and climbs past the Doyle River Cabin Spring (D) and reaches the *AT* (E) in 0.9 mi. (1.4 km.) from the Browns Gap Fire Road. Turn left and follow the *AT* south for 3.3 mi. (5.3 km.) to the beginning of the circuit (A).

# 19 *Hike No. 19*
# AUSTIN MTN.-FURNACE MTN.

*Circuit:* 11.6 mi. (18.7 km.); 6 hrs. 15 min.
*Side Trails:* 7.0 mi. (11.3 km.); 3 hrs. 45 min.
*Total:* 18.6 mi. (30.0 km.); 10 hrs. 0 min.
*Map Direction:* (A-B-C-D-E-F-G-H-I-J-K-A)

This is a long hard trip and is recommended for the seasoned hiker. The description is written for a start at Browns Gap (A) (MP 83). It circles in counterclockwise direction to Austin Mtn. and down into Madison Run Valley. The circuit climbs to Trayfoot Mtn. ridge by way of the Furnace Mtn. Trail. From there the route leads to Black Rock Mtn. with its excellent views and then by way of the *AT* back to Browns Gap. The basic circuit is 11.6 mi. (18.7 km.) with a total elevation change of approximately 2490 ft. (759 meters). Additional mileage is added if the hiker attempts to add all the side trails. The total then becomes 18.6 mi. (29.9 km.) with an approximated total elevation change of 4754 ft. (1449 meters).

Begin the hike at Browns Gap (A) and follow the *AT* north for 0.6 mi. (1.0 km.) to the top of the rise (B). Turn left onto the Big Run Trail. There is a slight rise then descent for 0.7 mi. (1.1 km.) to the junction of four trails in a gap (C). Continue ahead across the gap and follow the Rocky Top Trail (blue-blazed) for 0.4 mi. (0.6 km.) Turn left onto the Austin Mtn. Fire Trail (D) (yellow blazed). This trail descends down into a sag at 1.8 mi. (2.9 km.) (E). Turn left. (Straight ahead a side trail leads 0.35 mi. (0.6 km.) to the summit of Austin Mtn.)

Continue the descent following a very rough trail through a rocky area. *Important.* After descending 0.8 mi. (1.3 km.) there is a very sharp switchback to the left. A yellow-blazed side trail goes straight ahead from the apex of this switchback. It is possible to take the side trail and not notice that the main trail has made the left turn. The side trail dead ends in 0.2 mi. (0.3 km.) after reaching the ridge. No view.

Continue steep descent and reach the Madison Run Fire Road (F) after 3.2 mi. (5.2 km.) on the Austin Mtn. Trail. (To the left up Madison Run Fire Road it is 4.4 mi. (7.1 km.) to the beginning at Browns Gap (A).)

The circuit turns right and descends along Madison Run. In 0.6 mi. (1.0 km.) turn left onto the Furnace Mtn. Fire Trail (G) (yellow-blazed). Cross the stream and immediately turn right down stream. The trail is somewhat obscured by summer growth along the stream but soon veers away from the stream and then the route of the trail becomes unmistakable. Ascend and in 1.3 mi. (2.1 km.) the Furnace Mtn. side trail (H) (yellow-blazed) goes to the left. (This leads 0.45 mi. (0.7 km.) to an excellent view across Madison Run Valley toward Austin Mtn.)

From the junction with the Furnace Mtn. side Trail continue to ascend to a four way junction (I) in another 1.0 mi. (1.6 km.). The circuit turns sharply to the left. (The Abbott Ridge Fire Trail (yellow blazed) goes right. This trail is 1.1 mi. (1.8 km.) long. Good view from the end.) (The Hall Mtn. Fire Trail (yellow blazed) goes straight ahead across the intersection, south. It leads, very roughly, 1.3 mi. (2.1 km.) to excellent views.)

Continue climbing and in 3.0 mi. (4.8 km.) from Madison Run reach the Trayfoot Mtn. Fire Road (J). Turn left. (To the right the road climbs steeply to the summit of Trayfoot Mtn., (no views) in 0.2 mi. (0.3 km.). Limited views from stairway of lookout tower.)

Descend along the road for 0.5 mi. (0.8 km.) and in sag look for a short-cut trail (no signpost) going to the left and paralleling the road. Follow this trail, uphill, to the *AT* at Black Rock Mtn. (K). (If the shortcut is missed the Fire Road crosses the *AT* in 0.4 mi. (0.6 km.). Turn left.)

Follow the *AT* north from Black Rock Mtn. and reach Browns Gap (A) in 2.4 mi. (3.9 km.).

This circuit can also be reached from the Shenandoah

Valley. Drive to Grottoes, VA, on US 340. Take Virginia Secondary Road No. 663 to the east. Pass 629 and 708 coming in from the left, north. At the next road (private-no number), park. The Madison Run Fire Road continues ahead to the Park boundary where it is chained. There is no place to turn around or wide enough for parking, so do not drive beyond the suggested parking place. Hike up the road and reach the Park boundary in 0.2 mi. (0.3 km.) and the Furnace Mtn. Trail (G) in 0.1 mi. (0.2 km.) farther.

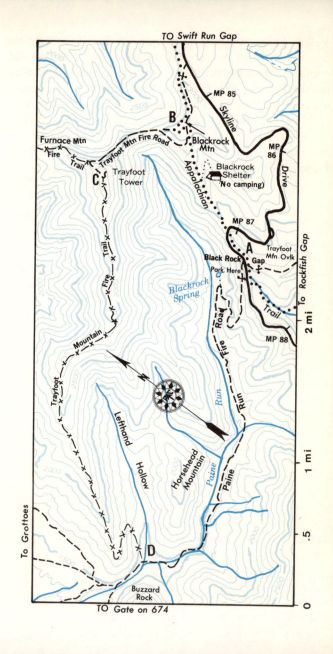

# 20 Hike No. 20
# TRAYFOOT MOUNTAIN

9.4 mi. (15.1 km.); 5 hrs. 15 min.
*Map Direction:* (A-B-C-D-A)

This circuit climbs to Black Rock Mtn. with its excellent view, climbs Trayfoot Mtn. and descends to Paine Run along the Trayfoot Mtn. Ridge, and returns by way of Paine Run Fire Road.

Black Rock Mtn. gets its name from the black appearance of the rocks caused by the lichen growing on them. Trayfoot Mtn. is conspicuous from the Skyline Drive but the trees around the fire tower have been allowed to grow up so that there is only a limited view. The Trayfoot Mtn. Ridge down which the trail descends has several good lookout points.

The highest point on the circuit is about 3360 ft. (1024 meters) just below the summit of Trayfoot Mtn. The low point is at Paine Run. 1420 ft. (433 meters). Total elevation change on the circuit is 2170 ft. (661 meters).

To begin the hike, park at Black Rock Gap (A) between MP 87 and 88. Cross to the east side of the Drive and hike north along the *AT*. The Drive is crossed again in a short distance and the *AT* climbs steadily. In 0.7 mi. (1.1 km.) the sidetrail to Black Rock Shelter leads right. Overnight use prohibited except in inclement weather.

Continue climb and at 1.2 mi. (1.9 km.) from the start cross the Trayfoot Mtn. Fire Road. This road leads left to the summit of Trayfoot Mtn. The circuit continues ahead on the *AT* and reaches Black Rock Mtn. (B) in another 0.1 mi. (0.2 km.). Excellent year round views. Find a trail to the left (well defined and maintained but no signpost). Turn left. Descend to gap and come into the Trayfoot Mtn. Fire Road. Ascend along the fire road. Pass the Furnace Mtn. Trail (yellow-blazed) leading right at 0.8 mi. (1.3 km.) from Black Rock Mtn. Continue climbing to the top of the ridge. Where the fireroad turns sharply to the left (C) to go to the firetower the Trayfoot Mtn. Fire Trail (yellow-blazed) leads right along the ridge. Turn right onto this trail. It may be overgrown at the start but soon develops into a well defined trail.

Descend along the Trayfoot Ridge. Reach Paine Run Fire Road (D) 3.8 mi. (6.1 km.) from Trayfoot Mtn. Turn left and climb via the Paine Run Fire Road back to Black Rock Gap (A) in 3.5 mi. (5.6 km.). About a mile before the Skyline Drive is reached a trail leads left at a sharp right bend in the fireroad. This reaches, in about 200 yds. (180 meters), Black Rock Spring. The spring was once regarded as a radium spring with medicinal properties.

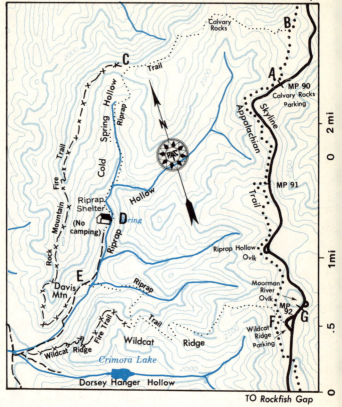

# 21 Hike No. 21
# RIPRAP HOLLOW

9.3 mi. (15.0 km.); 5 hrs. even.
*Map Direction:* (A-B-C-D-E-F-A)

This circuit uses the Riprap Trail and the *AT*. The Riprap Trail leads down into Riprap Hollow passing Calvary Rocks and Chimney Rock enroute. The beautifully located Riprap Shelter with its small swimming hole is passed and the trail climbs back to the *AT* via Wildcat Ridge. The *AT* is then followed north to the beginning of the circuit. Total elevation change is 2030 ft. (619 meters).

This hike can be started at either (A) the Calvary Rocks Parking Area (a few feet north of MP 90) or at (G) the Wildcat Ridge Parking Area (just south of MP 92). The description is from the Calvary Rocks Parking Area.

To begin the hike, park at the Calvary Rocks Parking Area (A) and follow a side trail for about 100 yds. (90 meters) to the *AT*. Turn right (north) and climb for 0.4 mi. (0.6 km.). At the junction with the Riprap Trail (B) (signpost) turn left. This trail first descends, then climbs around Calvary Rocks, then descends to Chimney Rock. Continue descent and pass the Rocks Mountain Fire Trail (C) (yellow-blazed) leading right at 1.8 mi. (2.9 km.). (This trail goes 3.0 mi. (4.8 km.) down to the Riprap road at a point about 0.8 mi. (1.3 km.) below Riprap Shelter. If this trail is followed, the hiker should turn left at the bottom to join the Riprap Trail in 0.2 mi. (0.3 km.).)

Pass Riprap Shelter (D) across the stream at 3.0 mi. (4.8 km.). Camping in inclement weather only. Small swimming hole.

Continue down the trail which soon comes into the old Riprap Road. At 0.6 mi. (1.0 km.) below the shelter the trail turns left (E) (concrete signpost) and crosses the stream. The trail soon begins climbing. Reach Wildcat Ridge at 4.5 mi. (7.2 km.). Turn left. The Wildcat Ridge Fire Trail comes in from the right. The Riprap road is 1.6 mi. (2.6 km.) down this trail. Overgrown in summer.

Continue climb and reach the *AT* (F) at 6.2 mi. (10.0 km.) from the start of the hike. Turn left (north) onto the *AT*. The Riprap Trail continues ahead across the *AT* and reaches the Skyline Drive at the Wildcat Ridge Parking Area (G) in 0.1 mi. (0.2 km.). The circuit can be started here.

Follow the *AT* for 2.7 mi. (4.3 km.) back to the start of the circuit (A).

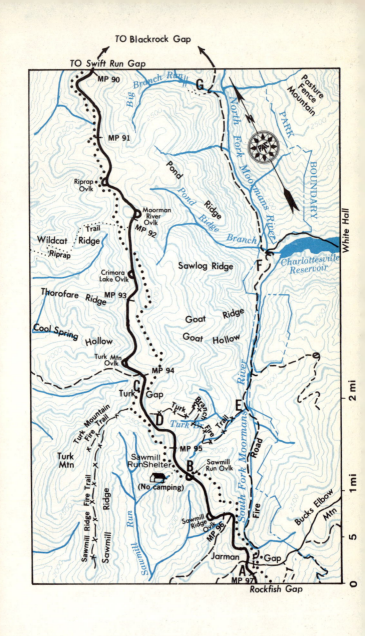

## 22 Hike No. 22
# TURK BRANCH-MOORMANS RIVER

*Short Circuit:* 8.6 mi. (13,8 km.); 4 hrs. 20 min.
*Long Circuit:* 20.8 mi. (33.5 km.); 8 hrs. 20 min.
*Map Direction:* (A-B-C-D-E-A) (off map)

This is a moderate length hike which can be lengthened to over 20 miles by those wanting a longer trip. The described circuit starts at Jarmans Gap (A) (between mileposts 96 and 97) and follows the *AT* north to Turk Gap (C) and descends (south) on the Skyline Drive for a short distance to pick up the Turk Branch Fire Trail (D). This trail leads down to the South Fork of Moormans River (E). The circuit turns right here and climbs back to Jarmans Gap via the Moormans River Fire Road. A side trip to Turk Mtn. is recommended and also a longer side trip to Charlottesville Reservoir and the Fall on Big Branch are very worthwhile.

Begin the hike at Jarmans Gap (A) and descend the Moormans River Fire Road (chained) and in 0.1 mi. (0.2 km.) reach the *AT*. Turn left onto the *AT* and descend along Moormans River; just a spring branch here. The trail begins a long steady climb after 0.5 mi. (0.8 km.). After gaining about 500 ft. (158 meters) in elevation, the trail descends to Skyline Drive (B) and crosses it at the north end of the Sawmill Run Overlook (MP 95-96). Climb and pass the Sawmill Run Shelter Trail at 1.9 mi. (3.1 km.). This trail leads left downhill, to the shelter. Camping is permitted only in inclement weather. The spring is unreliable in dry weather. The Turk Mtn. Fire Trail comes in from the left at 3.2 mi. (5.2 km.).

(The Turk Mtn. Fire Foot Trail leads west to the summit of Turk Mtn. in 1.1 (1.8 km.). Fine view. Look for fossilized worm holes in the rock at the summit. Enroute to Turk Mtn. the Sawmill Ridge Fire Trail, recommended for exploration only, leads south for 1.8 mi. (2.9 km.) and dead ends.)

Continue on the *AT* and reach Turk Gap (C) at 3.4 mi. (5.5 km.) just south of milepost 94. Turn right (south) along the Drive. Follow the Drive for 0.3 mi. (0.5 km.). On the left (east) side look for entrance to the Turk Branch Fire Trail (D) (yellow-blazed). Descend on this and after 1.9 mi. (3.1 km.) reach the Moormans River Fire Road (E). The circuit turns right here and follows the dirt fire road for 3.0 mi. (4.8 km.) to Jarmans Gap (A) and the end of the short circuit.

This hike can be extended by turning left (north) at the bottom of the Turk Branch Trail (E) and going down the Moormans River Fire Road for 1.9 mi. (3.1 km.) to the Charlottesville Reservoir (F). To extend the hike another 1.9 mi. (3.1 km.) continue to follow the fire road up the North Fork of Moormans River to Big Branch (G). A well defined trail, unmarked, leads left for 0.1 mi. (0.2 km.) to reach the waterfall. Return by the same route past the reservoir and join the shorter circuit at the bottom of Turk Branch and continue to Jarmans Gap (A).

*For a still longer circuit* the *AT* and the Moormans River Fire Road can be used to make a circuit of 20.8 mi. (33.5 km.). Begin at Jarmans Gap (A) and descend to the *AT*. Follow the *AT* north for 11.2 mi. (18.0 km.) to Black Rock Gap. (The northern portion of this long circuit is not shown on the map in this book, but see PATC Map No. 11 for Black Rock Gap.) Turn right (east) and descend the Moormans River Fire Road. Follow the fire road for 9.4 mi. (15.1 km.) back to Jarmans Gap. The short trail to Big Branch waterfall (G) and the Charlottesville Reservoir (F) are passed on this circuit.

The total elevation change on this longer circuit is 3520 ft. (1073 meters). Persons contemplating this trip should be capable of a sustained 2 1/2 miles per hour for an 8 hr. 20 min. (walking time) trip.

The hikes described can also be reached from outside the Park by following Virginia Secondary Road 810 from Crozet, VA, to White Hall and taking VA. 614 west to the Charlottesville Reservoir (F).